Beating the Paycheck to Paycheck Blues

John Ventura

Dearborn
Financial Publishing, Inc.®

Executive Editor: Bobbye Middendorf
Managing Editor: Jack Kiburz
Project Editor: Karen A. Christensen
Cover Design: Scott Rattray, Rattray Design
Interior Design: Lucy Jenkins
Typesetting: Elizabeth Pitts

97 98 99 10 9 8 7 6 5 4 3 2 1

Library of Congress Cataloging-in-Publication Data

Ventura, John
    Beating the paycheck-to-paycheck blues / John Ventura.
      p. cm.
    Includes bibliographical references and index.
    ISBN 0-7931-2325-9 (pbk.)
    1. Finance, Personal. 2. Consumer credit. I. Title.
HG179.V458 1997
332.024—dc20   96-36018
                                       CIP

DEDICATION

To Mary Ellen, my wife, with love

BOOKS BY JOHN VENTURA

The Bankruptcy Kit

Beating the Paycheck-to-Paycheck Blues

The Credit Repair Kit

The Small Business Survival Kit

The Will Kit

CONTENTS

PREFACE

*"A*dversity reveals genius, prosperity conceals it."

Horace (65–8 B.C.)

This book teaches you how to gain and maintain control of your financial life when you're singing the paycheck-to-paycheck blues. It shows you how to live successfully when you need to make every dollar count; how to improve your financial situation; and how to handle your debts and obligations if they get the best of you and serious money troubles develop.

Based on news reports, economic statistics, and the trends I've observed in my own bankruptcy law practice, a lot of you are singing the paycheck-to-paycheck blues:

- You're the victim of a corporate merger or downsizing and you're having trouble finding a well-paying job; your severance money is almost used up and you don't have much in savings.
- You've lost your job and have settled for a new one paying only a fraction of what you used to make; you can barely pay your bills. (According to a recent *New York Times* article, only about 35 percent of the full-time workers who have lost their jobs have been able to find new jobs that pay them as well or better than what they once earned.)
- Your job situation hasn't changed, but your income isn't keeping pace with your expenses.
- Your income is good and your job is stable, but you've taken on too much debt.
- You love being self-employed, but it's tough paying the bills on an irregular and unpredictable income.

- You've always lived paycheck to paycheck. So what else is new!

Former upper management executives who used to pull down six-figure salaries; blue-collar workers; professionals with graduate degrees; consumers who got only as far as high school—you all sing the blues these days! Yet despite your diversity, it's likely that you experience many of the same worries and concerns. For example, you feel a tremendous amount of anxiety about your family's financial well-being and how to pay the bills. You're sometimes overwhelmed by self-doubt and a sense of failure: This wasn't what you planned for your life; what did you do wrong? You lose sleep at night worrying about things like: What will I do if an expensive emergency develops? Will I be able to send my kids to college? And what about my retirement? Maybe the thought of bankruptcy has entered your mind for the first time.

Anxiety about financial well-being has become an American experience, shared by nearly everyone except those at the very top of the corporate ladder. Although the stock market may be reaching record highs and although the government tells us that these are good economic times, many of us aren't feeling so prosperous or confident. And although none of us can predict the future, current trends indicate that for a growing number of American workers, job security, good raises, and many other employment benefits are things of the past. Increasingly, it's up to us to create our own economic security.

Living successfully when money is tight and creating a brighter financial future for yourself and your family require that you take control of your finances, make every dollar count, and place less emphasis on material possessions. They also require a positive can-do attitude, which can be tough when you're worried about money and your prospects for the future.

Beating the Paycheck-to-Paycheck Blues provides you with much of the information you need to meet these challenges; it won't tell you what to do with your mutual funds or your 401(k); you can find plenty of books, magazines, and financial advisers to give you that advice. By reading this book, you will acquire very basic information and skills that can help you manage your finances—things you probably never learned in high school or college or from your parents. When your paychecks always came on a regular basis and credit was readily available, not having this knowledge probably didn't matter very much. In fact, you may not even have been aware that your education was lacking. Living on a budget and making every penny count probably wasn't something that concerned you. But now, if things have changed, you've begun to realize that you don't know how to deal with your current financial situation or that you need to deal with it more successfully.

The information in this book is presented in two sections. The first provides the basic money management information, advice, and skills you need to help pay your bills when money is tight, to make informed decisions about money and credit, and to avoid problems with your creditors. Here's a sampling of some of the subjects it covers:

- Developing and maintaining a positive attitude about your financial situation
- Living on what you make—no matter how much that is
- Earning extra money
- Getting the most for your dollar
- Knowing your legal rights as a consumer

The second section is for those readers who begin having serious trouble paying their creditors and also for those whose credit histories have already been damaged by too many bills and too little money. The subjects it covers include the following:

- Recognizing the signs of financial trouble and what to do when it develops
- Diagnosing the underlying causes of your financial troubles
- Dealing with debt collectors when they start calling
- Understanding the importance of credit bureaus and credit reports and dealing with problems in your report
- Living without credit or with less credit
- Rebuilding your credit after serious money troubles, including bankruptcy

Beating the Paycheck-to-Paycheck Blues also includes a helpful list of resources you can use to learn more about these and other subjects.

Whether you struggle to make ends meet or simply want to downscale your financial life so you'll be prepared for anything, *Beating the Paycheck-to-Paycheck Blues* can teach you to be a wise money manager and show you how to live a happy, fulfilling life without earning a six-figure salary.

ACKNOWLEDGMENTS

To Karen Christensen, whose attention to detail and concern for getting everything just right has contributed so much to this book and to my other ones. Plus to Anita Constant, my publisher, who is wise, perceptive, and kind enough to take time out of her busy day to talk with me whenever I call to talk about my books. And to Mary Reed, my friend and writing partner, who worked harder than anyone to bring this book to fruition and to make it a success.

ONE

Feeling Good When Things Are Bad

"The witch doctor succeeds for the same reason all the rest of us succeed. Each patient carries his own doctor inside himself. They come to us not knowing that truth. We are best when we give the doctor who resides within each patient a chance to go to work."

Albert Schweitzer

I hardly recognized Sid and Marla M. when they came to see me. A year before, I had met with them when they were going through an especially difficult time. Sid had lost his job, and they struggled to make ends meet on Marla's salary and any consulting work Sid could line up while he job hunted. The couple I remembered could hardly stand to be in the same room together during those stressful times.

Now here they were, making jokes about the past and obviously enjoying each other's company. I saw something in their relationship that I had not seen a year ago—respect for one another. They had stopped by to get some legal advice, but I was so amazed and curious about the change in their relationship that I asked them what had happened to make such a big difference.

1

"You're right," Sid said. "After I lost my job, it seemed like our financial world was collapsing around us, and Marla and I were under so much pressure that we could hardly stand to be together; in fact, we almost got a divorce. I was angry about what had happened to me, blaming everyone and everything for my misfortune, and I didn't think that Marla was being supportive enough. Fortunately, when things were the bleakest, we went to see our minister.

"His help had less to do with religion and more to do with common sense—something I was short of at the time. First he helped me get through the emotional upset of losing a job I loved and leaving the company I'd devoted years to. With his assistance, I came to realize that while my situation was not pleasant, I had control over how I chose to deal with it. Letting negative emotions take over was counterproductive to getting through the tough times. Our minister also suggested that Marla and I examine the roles that money and material possessions were playing in our lives. He said that if we placed less emphasis on those things, we might reduce the pressure we were feeling.

"Marla and I spent a lot of time thinking and talking about what our minister had said to us. We began to realize that throughout our marriage, driving new cars, wearing nice clothes, and owning a home in an expensive neighborhood were very important to us. To get those things, I had worked long hours at the expense of our family life and we had put very little in savings. We also started to talk about what made us happy, and we concluded that although we certainly had a good time spending money, the things that we found truly pleasurable and really valued cost little or nothing. Knowing that has made it much easier to live on less.

"That new perspective also gave me the freedom to take a job that paid me a lower salary than my previous job. Now I feel happier when I leave for work every day, and I have a lot more to give my family when I come home. Given our new attitude toward money, Marla and I are more content with our lives than we used to be, even though we don't have a lot of extra money to spend and we no longer use our credit cards unless we absolutely have to. In retrospect, losing my job and having to live on less were the best things that ever happened to us!"

As Marla and Sid discovered, your attitude can either help or hinder you when money is tight. The right attitude can help you get through difficult times and live a contented and happy life despite your economic constraints; the wrong attitude can create problems in your personal life and can even exacerbate your financial troubles.

This is not to say that it isn't a struggle when your paycheck barely covers your expenses or that all you need to keep financial disaster at bay is a good attitude. But the right perspective makes it easier for you to take control of your finances and to cope with your day-to-day ups and downs; plus it gives you the drive and energy you need to create a better future for you and your family.

Furthermore, knowing that you can live happily on less makes you ready for any challenge. And that self-knowledge increases your options in life and buys you a certain kind of financial freedom. When you realize that life can be a pleasure even if you don't have a lot to spend, you'll be less apt to end up tied to a job you hate just because it brings you a desired amount of money. Knowing that you can live well on less also prepares you to become self-employed—if that's your dream—because, as you probably know, entrepreneurs usually don't make much money when they first start out.

You may already have a can-do attitude about life and its adversities. Or you may need to develop that perspective. Sid and Marla did so with their minister's help. You may be able to do the same thing just by reading this book, or you may decide to talk with a close friend who shares your worries or with a counselor or therapist; you may even decide to join a group like Debtor's Anonymous.

Someone once said, "It's not the events of life that determine its quality; it's how you respond to those events." I have found that to be very true, and I hope the information in this and subsequent chapters helps you respond to the circumstances in your life in a manner that brings you happiness, new confidence, and belief in your future.

Recovering from Job Loss

"The longer we dwell on our misfortunes, the greater their power to harm us."

Voltaire

Many of you reading this book have lost your jobs. A year ago, life was good. You had all kinds of plans for how you would spend your money—a nice vacation, new furniture, maybe even an expensive car. Now those plans are gone, replaced by worries about how to pay your bills and whether you'll be able to find a job that pays close to what your old one paid.

Your concerns about the present and the future may be complicated by the emotions you feel. Those emotions may create additional stress in your personal life and get in the way of clear thinking and hope for the future.

People commonly experience a certain range of emotions after a major loss. Being aware of what those emotions are and knowing how to work through each of them are key to developing the attitude you need to leave the past behind, make the most of your present, and plan for the future. That attitude can mean the difference between your success and failure.

Shock

When you lose your financial security, your first response probably will be a sense of shock or disbelief. "How can this happen to me?" you may ask. The loss may shake your very core.

You may begin to question the fundamental truths and values upon which you've based your life. These might include: "If I work hard, pay my bills, and stay out of trouble, life will be good" or "Bad things happen only to bad people." When events in your life contradict long-held beliefs and assumptions, it's not uncommon to begin wondering whom and what to trust and what to believe in.

Although such doubt is often unpleasant, it's not necessarily bad. Fundamental upheaval can and should be treated as a chance to reexamine your lifestyle and your values, to test old assumptions, and to figure out what's really important to you. It's also an opportunity to change your life in positive ways. Your soul searching can result in benefits you never dreamed of and can open new doors in your life. Although what has happened may seem horrible at first, it in fact may end up being something wonderfully freeing and energizing. But before you can gain that perspective, you'll probably have to work through a few more emotions.

Anger

Feelings of anger commonly follow shock. You may begin looking for scapegoats for your troubles: big business, government, the politicians, your boss, your spouse, bad luck. Many people recovering from a major loss get stuck in this stage.

If you feel angry, allow yourself to express it, but direct it toward the situation, not toward scapegoats. Focusing on scapegoats is a nonproductive use of your energy and emotional resources and implies that you have no control over your life and that nothing you can do will make a difference. In fact, looking for scapegoats can cause you to lose confidence when you need it most.

Get angry. Acknowledge that something terrible has happened, and mourn what you have lost. Through anger, you can lay the groundwork for emotional healing and for building a new future.

Hot Tip

Research shows that painful events ultimately cause most people to discover more meaning in their lives. As Henry Ford once said, "Life is a series of experiences each of which makes us bigger even though sometimes it is hard to realize this."

Depression

You may also feel depressed after you lose your job, especially if you give in to feelings of guilt, anger, and anxiety. Soon you may find yourself feeling hopeless, helpless, and desperate, as though your life is falling apart.

Depression saps you of your energy and initiative—the very things you need to get your life back together. And giving in to it usually just makes you more depressed. Although some initial depression is certainly understandable when you lose something you value and perhaps enjoy, being depressed for a long period of time or being so depressed that you can't function keeps you tied to the past and unable to move forward.

When you feel depressed, remind yourself that you're not helpless and that you can improve your life. Take stock of all the good things in your life, and draw positive energy from them;

don't give in to self-pity or dwell on the bad. Here are some things you can do to help develop a positive attitude:

- *Acknowledge that you have responsibility for your own life and that you can make good things happen for yourself*—even if it requires a lot of effort and takes time.
- *Understand that the quality of your life is what's important, not the things that money can buy.* Think about the things in your life that give it quality—a loving spouse, happy children, good health, your surroundings, your friends.
- *Experience each day fully.* Don't dwell on the past or yearn for the future. Find something to enjoy or appreciate every day, even if it's something as simple as your child's smile or the sunset.
- *Surround yourself with the people you care about and enjoy being with.* As often as possible, put yourself in enjoyable situations that are free of stress.
- *Stay active.* Exercise, start a workout program, do yard work, or tackle a project in your home that you've wanted to do for a long time.
- *Get involved in a good cause.* Helping people less fortunate than yourself can put your situation in perspective and take your mind off your own troubles.
- *Pamper yourself.* Take a long, hot bubble bath, eat your favorite ice cream, listen to some good music.

If you're unable to shake your depression, you may need to seek professional help.

Resolution

Once you've experienced shock, anger, and depression and can confront the reality of what's happened in your life, you can begin moving forward. At this point in your emotional recovery, you probably will continue to experience some emotional ups and downs. Periodic feelings of anxiety, frustration, fear, and even anger are only normal, particularly when you feel financially vulnerable, perhaps for the first time in your life. So when you hit low points, don't get discouraged. Instead, remember the advice and information in this chapter, talk with your close friends and family members about what you're feeling, and move forward.

Maintaining a Positive Attitude

"I've never been poor, only broke. Being poor is a frame of mind. Being broke is only a temporary situation."

Mike Todd

People typically react to difficult challenges in one of two ways. Some respond, "Why is this happening to me?" They tend to view themselves as helpless victims of forces beyond their control. This perspective often triggers feelings of self-pity, frustration, and depression; rarely does it encourage productive problem solving. Often, as a result of their attitude, these people limit their access to the information and assistance that could help them deal more successfully with the challenges they face.

Other people recognize that life is a series of ups and downs. They believe that if things were good once, things can be good again and that *they* can make things better. They tend to have confidence in themselves and in their ability to take on difficult challenges. People with this attitude are more apt to seek out the resources that can help them achieve success and are open to testing new approaches toward life and living. They are not tied to their pasts.

As this chapter has already indicated, it's not always easy to feel positive and hopeful when money is tight. Yet that positive attitude is a powerful, necessary force when you are facing a difficult challenge. A negative attitude can be destructive. Here are some typical destructive attitudes:

- "I can't stand it when my life is out of control."
- "Why is everyone and everything ganging up on me? What did I do to deserve this?"
- "I can't do anything well; I'm a failure."
- "The present is awful, and I don't even want to think about the future."
- "I hate having other people know about my problems."

To maintain a positive attitude when you feel overwhelmed, worried, or disappointed by life, keep things in perspective. Recognize that as difficult as your life may be right now, other people have it worse. Also, remember that although it may not happen quickly and without sacrifice, you *can* change your life.

You *are* in control. Focus on the good things in your life; don't dwell on the negatives. Tell yourself the following, for example:

- "I am in control of my life. I can make things happen. I may not have as much money as I used to, but I still have my pride, my identity, my skills and knowledge, my friends, and my family."
- "The present is difficult, but the future can be better, and I can make it better."
- "I can learn lessons from my present troubles, and if I focus on these lessons, I can create a happier life for myself and my family."
- "Personal growth and development almost never happens when life is good; it is the challenges we face that make us better and stronger."

See Figure 1.1 for more ways to maintain a positive attitude.

Don't Give In to Guilt and Shame

"How can they say my life isn't a success? Have I not for more than 60 years got enough to eat and escaped being eaten?"
Logan Pearsall Smith

If you've lost your job or are having trouble making ends meet, it's easy to begin feeling guilt, embarrassment, and shame. If you do, depression may follow and you may have trouble moving forward. To help you keep your situation in perspective, consider the following:

- You're not the first person to lose your job, nor will you be the last. In fact, according to a *New York Times* analysis of Department of Labor data, since 1979, more than 43 million jobs have been eliminated. Many of these lost jobs are the result of our economy's restructuring and have nothing to do with the competence of those whose jobs have been eliminated.
- All kinds of people experience financial trouble—the rich and poor, the famous and not-so-famous, the financially responsible, and financially irresponsible. You're not the first person to worry about money, and you won't be the last!

FIGURE 1.1   Things You Can Do to Maintain a Can-Do Attitude

- Find reasons to laugh and smile.

- Each day, visualize a past success you achieved after much hard work.

- Envision your life six months from now, a year from now, and so on, and think about what you want to accomplish by those milestones.

- Get together with people who are in situations like yours—perhaps others who were laid off by your employer—and share ideas, encouragement, and leads.

- Make a list of all the positive things in your life right now.

- Make a list of all the people who have befriended you or helped you over the years. Each day, call or write one of them. Thank them for their kindness and offer to help them.

- Take the time to reestablish old friendships you may have neglected.

- Get involved in volunteer work. Helping others can help you keep your situation in perspective and make you feel good about yourself.

- Identify some important goals that you keep telling yourself you can't do because of fear, anxiety, or lack of money, for example. Challenge yourself to do them anyway, and find a way to accomplish them. For example, if you've stopped socializing with friends because you can no longer afford to have people over for dinner like you used to, invite your friends for pot-luck meals. Or if you have always feared public speaking, join the Toastmasters group in your area.

- Appreciate what you've done. Every time you make a major step toward achieving one of your goals, write it down in a diary or notebook. Or at the end of each week, look back on what you've accomplished and write it down. You may also want to record your goals for the coming week.

- Don't limit "something good" to things related to money. A beautiful sunset, a good conversation, and an enjoyable book are all "good things." Expanding your definition not only broadens your capacity for happiness and pleasure, it also helps you recognize that happiness is not necessarily something you buy.

- You're a failure only if you allow yourself to think like one. Stop to consider all of the people you hear about these days who are in the same boat as you are. Surely they are not all failures! Rather than dwelling on the mistakes you may have made or the disappointments you've experienced, think about what you've learned. Then act on that new knowledge. Remember, positive change and a brighter future can come out of hard times. Figure 1.2 highlights success stories from my own legal practice.

It's helpful to view a difficult situation as an opportunity, not as something to feel ashamed about. When you live paycheck to paycheck or lose your job, the opportunity may be to reexamine your values and priorities, to find more fulfilling work, to start a business, to go back to school, to create a more stable financial life, or to learn more about money management. Hard as it may be, try to find the positives in your situation; don't focus on the negatives. There *is* a silver lining in nearly every cloud!

Finally, if some of your friends ostracize you because you can't spend money like you used to, they really were never very good friends in the first place, and losing them is not a great loss. True friends stick by you.

Hot Tip _____

If you have friends or acquaintances who are dealing with money troubles, too, consider starting a support group. You can offer each other ideas for living frugally and making more money, trade job leads, and share ideas for starting your own businesses, beating stress, and coping with financial difficulties. Out of this sharing can come stronger friendships.

Rethink Success

When you struggle with money and especially if you used to make a substantial income and are bothered by the fact that you can't spend like you used to, consider rethinking your definition of success. You have many ways to define success besides the job

---

FIGURE 1.2   Overcoming Financial Difficulties

In my job, I often meet people who struggle to juggle their finances while they cope with major changes in their work situations, as well as people who recover from financial difficulty and use those struggles to create new and happier lives for themselves. A few success stories follow:

- A client of mine held a well-paying managerial position with a respected national company. He and his wife also ran a small business on the side, which helped pay for a nice vacation every year and other extras. After 20 years of working for his employer, my client lost his job when the company merged with another. He and his wife were devastated and consumed with worry about how they'd be able to pay the mortgage on their new home and other important bills. Their concern mounted after my client had met with some headhunters, who informed him that there was not a lot of demand for someone with his job skills. The headhunters suggested that he should be open to accepting work at a salary significantly less than he had been earning. However, after an initial period of depression and indecision, my client and his wife decided that she would take a part-time job, he would spend his days trying to make their business more successful, and at night, he would attend a local community college to increase his job skills. Today, after lots of hard work and sacrifice and little sleep, they feel a lot more confident. They've cut way back on their living expenses, and their business is beginning to thrive, thanks to the business management and computer skills my client acquired at night school. To top it all off, he and his wife spend more time together than they used to.
- Another client had a highly successful career as a well-paid executive in the retail clothing industry. But when the company she worked for merged with another, her position was eliminated. After months of financial struggle and job search, she had to file for bankruptcy. Undeterred, she took her knowledge of the clothing industry and began a home-based consulting business, selling her knowledge and experience to a number of upscale small and midsized retailers. Now she works out of a small office in her home, is more relaxed, and, after scaling back her spending, enjoys a very comfortable lifestyle.

FIGURE 1.2   Overcoming Financial Difficulties   (Continued)

- A successful commercial architect lost his job due to corporate cost cutting. Although he went on a number of job interviews, no one wanted to pay him what he used to make, and as time went on, he began to question whether he really wanted to return to the pressures and responsibilities that would inevitably come with a six-figure salary. Therefore, he took some consulting work to help pay the bills and to buy himself some time to decide what he really wanted to do. After reading several career-planning books and meeting with a career counselor provided by his former employer, he began to think about how much he'd enjoyed working with students when he was a teaching assistant in graduate school. Therefore, he decided to change careers and today teaches drafting to high schoolers. He has never felt so fulfilled.

---

you hold, how much money you make, and the things you spend it on. Success also can be considered having a happy relationship with your spouse or partner, raising well-adjusted, loving children, making a difference in the lives of others, having a life rich with friends, living with peace and joy, and sticking to your convictions and values. These are all things that money can't buy!

Remember, many people who have had successful careers and made a lot of money have never experienced much personal happiness. It may be trite to say, but money really *doesn't* buy happiness.

Set Goals and Work toward Them

"It is not enough to believe in something; you have to have the stamina to meet obstacles, to overcome them, to struggle."

Golda Meir

It's important to establish goals for yourself and to work toward them when you're struggling to pay your bills and maybe trying to recover from job loss as well. Doing so will help reinforce the fact that you *do* have control over your life and that you *can* do things to improve it. Your progress can also help stave off depression.

What you're able to accomplish at first may seem small and insignificant given your overall goals. However, don't let that stop you—do what you can. Little by little, step by step, you *will* make progress. Each series of little steps adds up to big steps.

As you analyze what you need to do to achieve your goals, don't allow yourself to become overwhelmed. Break each problem or challenge into small, doable tasks, and accomplish one at a time.

Hot Tip

Use a sport like biking, swimming, or jogging to overcome feelings of anxiety or depression. Intense absorption in a physical activity that requires you to focus on the present can help take your mind off your worries and can make you feel good about yourself and more hopeful about the future. Intense exercise is also energizing.

Draw Strength from Friends and Family

When you're stressed out about money, it's easy to direct your anger and frustration at other people—often your friends and family—the very people you need most during difficult times. You may find that you push people away from you, creating even more stress in your life. A better way of dealing with your stress is to be open and honest with your friends and family about what you feel and what you worry about. This approach is less apt to alienate or anger them.

It can also help to write about your emotions or even talk about them on tape. Professional counseling is often a good idea, too. If you can't afford a private counselor, a nonprofit organization in your area or your local or state health department may offer such services free of charge or at a reduced price or know where you can get them.

Another good idea is to call regular family meetings to talk about the changes that have taken place in your life and their possible impact on your family's financial well-being. Ask everyone for his or her patience and support, and encourage everyone to ask questions. If necessary and appropriate, use your family meetings to apologize for any rude or difficult behavior on your part and to assure your family that you love them. Don't forget, if you've lost your job or are having trouble making ends meet, your children probably feel some anxiety; talking about their feelings and getting reassurance from you can help them.

Do the same with your close friends. Maintaining an open and honest dialogue with your friends and family can make you feel better about the challenges you face and encourages the important people in your life to provide you with the comfort and support you may need.

Some of your friends and extended family also may be having a tough time making ends meet, but they may have been reluctant to talk about their troubles. By opening up to them, you encourage them to share their problems, worries, hopes, and dreams with you.

Not only can such sharing be emotionally beneficial, but it can have immediate, practical benefits. For example, you can trade job leads, and share ideas for cutting your expenses, fun things to do on a budget, and resources for starting a business.

Children and Money Worries

If you're a parent, a major problem you may face when you try to tighten your belt is how to deal with the kids. This can be a particular problem if you used to make a good income and your children are accustomed to having pretty much whatever they want. Should you pretend that money isn't a problem? Or should you be honest—and if so, just how honest?

Most experts agree that it's usually best for your children to have at least a general understanding of your family's financial situation. Sensing that things are different, but not being sure of why and exactly how the change in your family's finances will affect them can create tremendous anxiety in your children. However, use your judgment regarding just how much to tell them. Remember, every child is different, and like adults, each child has a different capacity for dealing with change and stressful situations. See Figure 1.3 for possible reactions to your news.

Generally, you can be more forthcoming with your preteen and teenage children than you can with younger children. You can explain why and how things have changed or how they will

---

FIGURE 1.3   Common Reactions of Children to Difficult Changes
in Their Lives

Your children may demonstrate no obvious reaction to the decrease
in your household income, to your job loss, or to any other troubles
your family experiences. However, depending on their ages, your children may respond in one or more of the following ways:

Younger Children

- Bad dreams
- Return to more infantile behaviors
- Excessive crying or clinging

Older Children

- Anger
- Discipline problems in school or at home
- Use of drugs or alcohol

---

change and what you're doing about the situation. Reassure
them that as a family, you can deal with the change. Most likely,
your children will be anxious to help however they can.

Younger children may not be able to understand exactly what
is going on in your lives and may be more prone to misinterpret
what you tell them. However, if your financial struggles will affect them in direct ways that they will notice—no more private
music lessons or fewer new clothes, for example—they deserve a
general explanation of the changes in your family's financial circumstances. Be careful not to say anything that will scare them,
however.

One way to alleviate the fear or stress children may feel if
money has become tight is to tell them about other families they
may know who also live paycheck to paycheck. Knowing that
they're not alone can reassure your children, no matter what their
ages, and can encourage them to talk openly with their friends
about what's happening.

Consider making your children part of the solution. For example, ask your older children for their ideas about how to reduce household expenses and where they might cut back—
perhaps they could get along on smaller allowances, for example.

An older high school student might be asked to help out by getting a temporary, part-time job after school or on weekends, as long as it won't interfere with studies. Also, if you and your spouse both begin working to bring in more money, ask your children to help more with household chores like cooking and cleaning.

Peer pressure can be particularly difficult for your children to deal with. That their friends are able to do things that your children used to do too can make them angry, resentful, or embarrassed. This problem has no easy solution. Let your children know that you realize it may be difficult for them right now, but that everyone in your family is making sacrifices. And remind them of all the things they do have in their lives.

You may want to suggest ways that your children can earn extra money to buy some of the things they want. Also, show them how to get the most for their money by taking them to discount stores, resale shops, and garage sales and by teaching them how to read the newspaper classifieds. Help them develop healthy attitudes about money!

Hot Tip

Help your children develop healthy perspectives about money and material possessions. Understanding that people should be valued and judged for who they are and the good things they accomplish in life, not for what they wear, drive, or buy, is an invaluable lesson. This understanding will help your children be less subject to pressure from their peers.

When things have changed for your family, it's more important than ever to spend special time every week alone with each of your children; try to do something as a family as well. Use your time together to have fun and to show affection. This time can be especially important if your financial situation has forced you to cut back on lessons or activities that your children once enjoyed. Time together can reassure them that some things in their lives have not changed—your love and their sense of family.

Stress Busters

Money troubles can bring stress. Feeling stress is normal when you're worried about your bills and about how your financial situation may affect your children and your relationship with your spouse.

If you feel too much stress, you may have trouble sleeping and thinking clearly, and you may be more prone to illness. Therefore, if stress interferes with your ability to cope and to move forward, consider some of the following stress beaters:

- Exercise regularly; sweat your stress away!
- Read a good book.
- Take up yoga, or learn to meditate.
- Play with your children.
- Spend time with friends.
- Listen to relaxing music.
- Garden.
- Rediscover nature. (Take walks in the woods, listen to the sounds of nature, smell the great outdoors, admire the sunset or the sunrise.)
- Take up an inexpensive hobby.
- Get involved in a worthy cause.
- Get plenty of sleep. Feeling rested makes it easier to deal with whatever comes your way, calmly and sensibly. Lack of sleep can make you more subject to stress and can affect your decision-making ability.

Not only can these stress beaters help you relax, they can contribute to a healthier, happier, spiritually richer, more balanced life as well.

Dealing with the Holiday Season

Even when you're not concerned about money and everything is going well in your life, the December holidays can be incredibly stressful. Whether you celebrate Christmas, Hanukkah, Kwanzaa, or the winter solstice, the pressure to give presents and to entertain can be intense at this time of year. So not being able to spend as much money as you used to during the holidays can make you feel guilty.

However, being strapped for cash doesn't automatically mean you and your family can't have a happy, joyful holiday season. Once again, it's all in your attitude!

When money is tight, you and your family have an opportunity to rediscover the true spirit and forgotten pleasures of a simpler, bygone era—something many of us yearn for now that the holiday season has become so commercial. You can turn the clock back to a time when the holidays were about giving homemade gifts and gifts from the heart, relaxing with family and friends, caroling, and doing something special for those less fortunate—simple pleasures that can have great meaning.

The key to creating an old-fashioned (or perhaps *new-fashioned*) holiday season is to shift your family's focus away from what they can buy and receive, away from the cost or trendiness of presents, and toward the sentiment and thought behind gifts. New-fashioned holidays don't mean an end to store-bought gifts and toys; but they place a greater emphasis on gifts from the heart: homemade gifts, gifts of one's time, thoughtful gestures and favors. This approach to the holidays not only creates a more relaxed and less expensive holiday season, but also teaches your children invaluable lessons about the true spirit and pleasure of giving.

This approach to gift giving works equally well for birthdays.

Blues Busters

Living paycheck to paycheck is never easy, especially if you're used to earning more. Worrying about how to pay your bills and what you'll do if an expensive emergency develops can be overwhelming. If your money troubles are due to the loss of your job, the emotions you may experience as a result can make coping especially difficult because depression, anger, and scapegoating can sap your energy and divert you from focusing on what is really important to you.

But with the right attitude and a lot of hard work, you can accomplish just about anything. I know this is true because I have worked with clients facing tremendous money troubles. The clients most apt to overcome their troubles and go on to create more financially secure lives for themselves are almost always the ones who refuse to give in to depression and negativity and who are determined to make the best of their current situations by focusing on the positives in their lives and by working toward the future. Although they may have periodic setbacks, they never stop believing in themselves and in their ability to triumph over adversity. To help you develop the attitude you need to beat the paycheck-to-paycheck blues, here are some final thoughts to remember when things seem especially difficult:

- You are more than the job you may have lost.
- You are a worthwhile person even if you no longer make the money you used to make.
- Your money and your job have nothing to do with your integrity as a human being.
- The truly important and lasting things in life have nothing to do with money and material possessions.
- You're not alone in your troubles.

TWO

Doing the Most with What You've Got

"Getting money is like digging with a needle. Spending it is like water soaking into sand."

Japanese proverb

Howard and Jean H. were facing financial troubles and an uncertain future. Six months ago, Howard had lost his job after working for his employer for 15 years. He had joined the company after getting a graduate degree and over the years had received a series of promotions and seen his income rise steadily. During that time, Howard and Jean spent what they wanted. They purchased an expensive home in a nice neighborhood, joined a country club, took nice vacations, and gave their three children the best of everything. Although Jean worked during the early years of their marriage, she had not been employed outside the home in a number of years.

Howard was emotionally devastated by his sudden job loss. He felt betrayed by the company that he had worked so hard for. But after a month of moping around the house, he decided it was time to find another job. He had received a severance package from his former employer that would take care of his family's expenses for about six months, and Howard was confident that with his experience and qualifications, he'd be able to find a good position pretty quickly. But as the months passed, Howard and Jean began to worry. The money they had in the bank was dwindling, and Howard had no good job offers.

Then Howard had an interview with a small, up-and-coming business that had been in operation for a little more than a year. The company president was looking for someone with Howard's talents, but could not offer Howard the compensation package he'd enjoyed at his old company. Even so, Howard was tempted. He was excited by the success that the company had enjoyed so far and was intrigued by the opportunities that working for the firm presented. However, he and Jean worried about how they would be able to live on less, especially because their oldest child would attend college at the end of the year and their second child would be college age in another two years. And then they had their retirement to think about.

Howard and Jean scheduled an appointment with me to discuss what to do. Although Jean planned to return to work to help out with their bills, they never before had to watch the way they spent money, and they realized that even with Jean's income, they would have to downscale their lifestyle and learn how to manage their money. But they didn't know the fundamentals of money management. Their parents never helped them develop those skills, and they didn't learn them in school. Therefore, they hoped I could provide them with some practical information about how to live on less and how to make the most of their money. I gave them some handouts on creating a budget (or spending plan) and told them about some books I felt would be worthwhile for them to read. I also referred them to several local organizations that sponsored low-cost money management seminars.

I told Howard and Jean that they must begin managing their money very differently than they had in the past. Although the long-term outlook was bright for the company Howard would work for, to get through the next several years, they needed to cut their living expenses, pay off their debt, and make every dollar count. Doing so would require that Howard, Jean, and their children make financial sacrifices and changes in their lifestyles. Most important, Howard and Jean must learn to be smart money managers.

This chapter and many of the chapters that follow provide much of the basic information consumers like Howard and Jean need when they try to make ends meet. If you think you need to raise your financial IQ, read other books and magazines. (The "Resources" section at the end of this book provides suggestions for more readings.) In addition, consider taking a money management class at your local community college or attending low-cost or no-cost seminars on the basics of money management. Ask your banker about them, or call your area's Consumer Credit Counseling Service (CCCS) office; this office may offer money management seminars or know who does. If you don't see a CCCS office listing in your local phone directory, call the national office at 800-388-2227. Ask for the CCCS office closest to you. Also, if you work with a financial adviser or money manager, take a more active role in your financial affairs.

The Importance of a Spending Plan

"If you have built castles in the air, your work need not be lost; that is where they should be. Now put the foundations under them."
                                                    Henry David Thoreau

A spending plan, better known as a budget, is an essential money management tool and key to living within your means. Developing and living with a spending plan can be a challenge if you are used to spending whatever you want whenever you want. But when money is tight, having a written plan that helps you allocate your dollars to pay for essential expenses and for special things you want to do in the future is essential. It's your financial road map. Figure 2.1 provides an overview of the steps involved in developing a spending plan.

Your entire family should help develop your household spending plan because its success may require each person's active participation. Involving everyone in the family yields a number of benefits. First, everyone becomes more aware of how much things cost. Second, if everyone understands that the way he or she spends money can affect others, your family will be a stronger unit. Third, talking about your spending plan and how it's working gives your family a regular time—perhaps over dinner—to get together and talk. If your lives are like most people's today, everyone in your family is so busy with work, school, activities outside the home, and routine day-to-day chores that it's a rare occasion when you all sit down together, just to talk. Monthly or bimonthly spending plan meetings give you the chance to do that.

FIGURE 2.1   How to Develop a Spending Plan

Step #1. Establish your goals—that is, what you want your spending plan to help you achieve.

Step #2. Determine how you spend your money. Where does it go?

Step #3. Compare total monthly household expenses to net monthly household income.

Step #4. If your expenses exceed your income, target areas for reduction.

Step #5. If you have a surplus—that is, you make more than you spend—allocate the excess to your top priority goals.

Step #6. Record your spending plan, and give a copy to each member of your household.

Step #7. Monitor your spending, and modify your spending plan as necessary.

Another benefit of involving the whole family in a spending plan is that it provides you with an opportunity to teach your children valuable lessons about money management. That information will help them avoid financial problems when they're adults rather than having to learn those lessons through trial and error and sometimes emotionally painful and expensive mistakes.

Hot Tip

Teach your children about money management by being a positive role model. It may be a cliché, but actions *do* speak louder than words.

Involving your family in the development of a spending plan also increases the likelihood that everyone will commit to its success. A team approach is critical because making a spending plan work almost inevitably requires at least some changes and sacrifices in your family's lifestyle. If you're all involved, success is more likely.

Setting Financial Goals

The first step in developing a spending plan is one or more brainstorming sessions to establish your household's short-term and long-term financial goals. These sessions give you and your family an opportunity to dream a little bit. Each of you should ask yourself what you want to accomplish, or what you want to be able to afford, in six months, one year, two years, and so on. Possible goals might include getting out of debt within the next two years; saving $500 over the next year; buying a new computer within the next six months; taking a family trip to Disneyland two summers from now; or saving $3,000 over the next three years as a down payment on a house or for your children's college fund.

While each session should focus on household financial goals, each of you may also want to develop personal financial goals. These goals need not be discussed with other household members. However, if achieving a personal goal requires everyone's cooperation, move that goal to the list of household goals. For example, you or your spouse may want to go back to school to get new job skills to increase your household income. (This was something Jean decided to do so that Howard would feel less financial pressure.)

Paying for that schooling may mean that other members of your family will have to sacrifice in some way. For example, they may have to temporarily give up something extra that they enjoy or work at a second job. Also, if you are going to be busy studying during your free time, you may need family members to perform some of the household chores you're typically responsible for.

Discuss and evaluate all of the goals proposed during your brainstorming sessions. Drop those that seem unrealistic or have low priorities. Be prepared to compromise—some household goals will be important to everyone, but others will draw differing opinions.

Hot Tip

Post your list of household goals where everyone in your family can see it. Periodically indicate your progress in achieving a particular goal—for example, "$200 left to pay on credit card debt" or "as of September 15, $500 in savings." Motivate your household, and encourage everyone to stick to the spending plan.

Once you've decided on your goals, categorize them as either short term (six months to two years) or long term (more than two years). Prioritize them, making the most important or most immediately pressing goal your number one short-term goal. The one

FIGURE 2.2   Goal Planning Chart

Short-Term or Immediate Goals

Goal	Total Cost	Monthly Cost	Target Date
#1 _____	$ _____	$ _____	_____
#2 _____	$ _____	$ _____	_____
#3 _____	$ _____	$ _____	_____
#4 _____	$ _____	$ _____	_____

Long-Term Goals

Goal	Total Cost	Monthly Cost	Target Date
#1 _____	$ _____	$ _____	_____
#2 _____	$ _____	$ _____	_____
#3 _____	$ _____	$ _____	_____
#4 _____	$ _____	$ _____	_____

that is slightly less important becomes your number two short-term goal, and so on. Do the same with your long-term goals. Record each on a goal planning chart like the one in Figure 2.2.

It's probably not possible to work toward all of your goals at once, so prioritizing them can help isolate those goals that you should make a part of your spending plan from the start. Begin with the most important of your short-term goals. As you accomplish them, you can move other short-term goals to the top of your list and onto your spending plan, or you can accelerate your efforts to achieve a high-priority long-term goal, such as saving for your children's college educations or your retirement.

To the right of each high-priority goal in both the short-term and long-term categories, record a total cost, a monthly cost (the total cost of the goal divided by the number of months you have to achieve it), and your target date.

Analyzing Current Spending Patterns

As mentioned earlier, you must change your spending habits to achieve your goals. To pinpoint those changes, develop a detailed picture of your current spending patterns—how you spend your money now. Do this by using your check register, receipts, and other household expenditure information for the year so far and for the previous year. (If you use a computer software program to manage your finances, reviewing your spending patterns will be easy.) Identify total annual costs for your monthly expenses as well as for one-time or periodic expenses like appliance repairs, medical bills, insurance, clothing, car repairs, and taxes. Revise these totals if you feel they are no longer accurate given changes in your current situation. Then divide each total by 12 to calculate a monthly cost for each expense.

As you review your household expenses, organize them into categories: fixed monthly expenses, variable monthly expenses, periodic expenses, and "set asides." Fixed monthly expenses occur in the same amount each month. Variable monthly expenses occur each month in different amounts; they are expenses over which you have some discretion or control. Periodic monthly expenses occur throughout the year, but not necessarily monthly; they can be either fixed or variable. Set aside expenses are totally discretionary, such as savings or certain goals.

To develop a complete picture of your household's current spending patterns, identify all miscellaneous cash expenditures. The best way to do this is for each adult and older child in your household to record his or her daily cash expenditures in a small notebook for several weeks or long enough for everyone to get a clear idea of how he or she spends the money carried with that person each day. Keep track of everything, even the most incidental expense. (See Figure 2.3.) You'll be surprised to discover how much you spend on miscellaneous items and how those seemingly minor purchases can add up to a rather significant sum over a period of time. Consider this: if you spend an average of $5 each working day on lunch, snacks, and sodas, that translates into $100 each month, or $1,200 a year!

Don't wait until the end of the day to record your miscellaneous expenditures. Inevitably, you will overlook something or forget entirely to record the information. Use a notebook small enough to fit in your pocket or purse, and discipline yourself to record every cash expenditure at the time you make it. This may be difficult to do, but it will be worth it. You'll probably be surprised to see how much money you spend on incidentals.

FIGURE 2.3 Spending Plan Worksheet—Current Income and Expenses*

Calculating Household Expenses

Fixed Monthly Expenses	*$ Amount*
Rent or mortgage	$ _____
Car loan	_____
Other installment loans	_____
Insurance	_____
Allowances	_____
Day care	_____
Monthly dues	_____
Newspaper subscriptions	_____
Cable TV	_____
Medical, dental, and prescriptions (after insurance)	_____
Transportation	_____
Total Fixed Monthly Expenses	_____

Variable Monthly Expenses	*$ Amount*
Groceries and household products	$ _____
Utilities	_____
Telephone	_____
Gasoline	_____
Clothing	_____
Credit cards	_____
Cleaning and laundry	_____
Toiletries and makeup	_____
Medical, dental, and prescriptions (after insurance)	_____
Magazines and books	_____
Online computer use	_____
Meals out	_____
Entertainment and hobbies	_____
Cigarettes, candy, etc.	_____
Total Variable Monthly Expenses	$ _____

FIGURE 2.3   Spending Plan Worksheet—Current Income and Expenses*   (Continued)

Periodic Fixed and Variable Monthly Expenses	*$ Amount*
(Total annual expense ÷ by 12 months = Monthly cost for each periodic fixed or variable expense)	
Tuition	$ _____
Auto registration and license	_____
Insurance	_____
Taxes	_____
Haircuts	_____
Household repairs	_____
Clothing	_____
Birthdays and holidays	_____
Medical, dental, and prescriptions (after insurance)	_____
Subscriptions	_____
Total	$ _____
Set Asides	$ _____
Savings	$ _____
Total	$ _____
Total Monthly Expenses	$ _____
Net Monthly Income	$ _____
Surplus or Deficit (Income – Expenses)	$ _____

*Expenses listed here are not intended to represent an inclusive list of possible household expenses, but rather are examples of common expenses.

Using a spending plan worksheet similar to the one in Figure 2.3, record your household expenses in the appropriate categories. Total each category, and fill in the line labeled "Total Monthly Expenses" at the bottom of the worksheet.

Calculating Household Income

Now calculate the amount of your net monthly household income (your gross income less all deductions). Include in this total any rental income, child support, and retirement benefits that you receive regularly.

If your household income varies due to the type of work you or your spouse does, it will be harder to determine your net income. The best solution is to look at your net income for the past two or three years and average those figures together, assuming you feel the result is a fair representative of what you'll earn in the immediate future. If not, increase or decrease the averaged amount by however much more or less you expect to earn. Don't overestimate your added income. It's always better to be conservative and have an unexpected surplus in your spending plan than to be overly optimistic and end up with a shortfall. Record your net monthly income figure on the spending plan worksheet.

Pinpointing Areas for Reduction

After you've recorded your expense and income figures on the worksheet, subtract total expenses from total income. This gives you either a spending surplus or a spending deficit. If you have a surplus, it can be allocated toward one or more of your goals. If you have a deficit, however, you don't have enough money to cover all of your expenses, much less work toward any of your goals. That means you need to identify expenses you can reduce.

Everyone in your household should examine his or her own spending to identify expenses that can be reduced. Be realistic about where you can cut back, but don't develop such a stringent spending plan that you won't be able to live with it. At the same time, remember that the more you reduce, the easier it will be to achieve your goals.

Critically analyze each expense category listed on your spending plan worksheet, and go back over your spending notebooks. Your goal should be to get your total monthly expenses below your total net monthly income by the total amount you want to allocate to your goals each month. (Figure 2.4 provides tips on saving money.) As you think about where you might cut back, here are the kinds of questions your family should ask:

- Can we cut back on subscriptions?
- Is getting to work using public transportation or car pooling a realistic possibility?
- Could we move to less expensive housing?
- Can we do things to make more efficient use of our home's heating and air-conditioning system? (Call your local utility company for energy-saving tips.)

- How can we reduce our grocery bill? (Buying house brands is an option.)
- Can we rent videos rather than seeing first-run movies? Does a nearby theater run discount shows? Do we really need a movie channel or premium cable channels?
- Can we make greater use of the library or swap books and magazines with friends?
- Can we shop at discount houses, warehouse stores, and outlets?
- Can we reduce our insurance costs?

It's human nature to resist change, but change can be a positive force in our lives. It can help us make new discoveries about ourselves, our relationships, and the world around us. And those discoveries can have unexpected benefits. For example, although using public transportation or walking to work each day will help save on gas, tolls, parking, and wear and tear on your car, it also provides a quiet time for contemplation, reading, or just watching the world. Such times are rarities—they're worth being open-minded about.

Hot Tip _____

If you have a lot of credit card debt on multiple cards, consider consolidating that debt on a single, low-interest card. You'll save money on interest and fees, and it will be easier to remember to make one payment rather than multiple payments, so you'll be less apt to incur costly late fees. Other options include getting a debt consolidation loan or applying for a no-fee/low-fee, no-points/low-points equity line of credit.

Recording a Spending Plan

"Yesterday is a canceled check; tomorrow is a promissory note; today is the only cash you have—so spend it wisely."

Kay Lyons

Once you've identified the expenses you can reduce, record the new totals on your worksheet, calculate a new monthly expense total, and subtract it from your total monthly household income. If you can now fund at least all of your highest priority short-term goals, you're ready to finalize and begin using your spending plan.

FIGURE 2.4   How to Be Thrifty

Here are some tips for reducing expenses and keeping your spending within the limits of your spending plan:

- Make your children's school lunches.
- Start a vegetable garden.
- Clean your oven regularly for greater efficiency.
- Change or clean your air conditioner filters once a week during the cooling season.
- Keep your hot water heater thermostat at 120 degrees.
- Don't go to first-run movies, or go only during discount hours.
- Get a free or low-cost energy audit if your local utility offers one.
- Shop for the best deal on a long-distance telephone carrier. Discount providers can offer real savings.
- Use your town's public library.
- When you entertain, make it potluck.
- Use your public parks, and take advantage of free or low-cost community events.
- If you subscribe to magazines, pass them on to friends when you're finished reading them, and ask your friends to do the same.
- Instead of calling, write friends and relatives who live far away.
- Never grocery shop when you're hungry.
- Don't shop without a list.
- Buy paper products, cleaning supplies, and other household items in bulk whenever practical.
- Shop at discount and warehouse stores.
- Plan your clothing purchases. At the start of every season, look at your clothes, and decide what you need to buy. When you purchase an item of clothing, make sure it will coordinate with as much of your wardrobe as possible. Avoid trendy items.
- Pump your own gas.
- Find out whether your bank allows banking by computer. If it does, you can save on many fees.
- Make sure you're getting the best deal on an Internet service provider. Local providers as well as some of the bigger long-distance carriers may offer better deals than your current provider.
- Shop at resale shops, outlets, garage sales, and used-book stores whenever possible.

FIGURE 2.4   How to Be Thrifty   (Continued)

- Swap clothing and jewelry with friends.
- Trade services with your neighbors and friends.
- Stop buying lottery tickets.
- Stop smoking. Not only will you save money, but you'll be on the road to better health, and you may be able to get your health insurance premium reduced.
- Call your insurance agent to discuss practical ways you can reduce the cost of your insurance premiums without jeopardizing your coverage.

Create a form similar to the chart in Figure 2.5; label it "Current Spending Plan"; write in your total monthly income; and fill in the amounts you've budgeted to spend each month. In the set aside category, record the specific goals you'll begin working toward and how much you'll allocate to them each month. Give each household member a copy of the spending plan.

If you still don't have enough money to fund your highest priority goals, you will have to reduce your spending still more, and you may also want to identify ways to increase your household income. For example, your older children may need to get part-time jobs, or you or your spouse may need to find a second job. For more ideas about increasing your household income, refer to Chapter 3.

Monitoring a Spending Plan

"Do what you can, with what you have, where you are."

Theodore Roosevelt

Once you've finalized your spending plan, you need to make it work. For that to happen, you must develop a good recordkeeping system, decide who in your household will be responsible for paying bills each month, and hold regular household meetings to monitor the plan and evaluate how well it is working.

Recordkeeping.   A good recordkeeping system can help you monitor your household income and expenditures. It can be as simple as a series of manila folders, labeled by category of

---

FIGURE 2.5 Current Spending Plan

Fixed Monthly Expenses	*$ Amount*
Rent or mortgage	$ _____
Car loan	_____
Other installment loans	_____
Insurance	_____
Allowances	_____
Day care	_____
Monthly dues	_____
Newspaper subscriptions	_____
Cable TV	_____
Medical, dental, and prescriptions (after insurance)	_____
Transportation	_____
Total	_____

Variable Monthly Expenses	*$ Amount*
Groceries and household products	$ _____
Utilities	_____
Telephone	_____
Gasoline	_____
Clothing	_____
Credit cards	_____
Cleaning and laundry	_____
Toiletries and makeup	_____
Medical, dental, and prescriptions (after insurance)	_____
Magazines and books	_____
Online computer use	_____
Meals out	_____
Entertainment and hobbies	_____
Cigarettes, candy, etc.	_____
Total	$ _____

FIGURE 2.5   Current Spending Plan (Continued)

Periodic Fixed and Variable Monthly Expenses	*$ Amount*
Tuition	$ _____
Auto registration and license	_____
Insurance	_____
Taxes	_____
Haircuts	_____
Household repairs	_____
Clothing	_____
Birthdays and holidays	_____
Medical, dental, and prescriptions (after insurance)	_____
Subscriptions	_____
Total	$ _____
Set Asides	$ _____
Savings	$ _____
Goal #1	_____
Goal #2	_____
Goal #3	_____
Total	$ _____
Total Monthly Expenses	$ _____
Net Monthly Income	$ _____
Surplus or Deficit (Income – Expenses)	$ _____

---

expense and income, and stored in a filing cabinet or box. A second file should be kept for bills to be paid.

Get receipts for all of your expenditures, and file them together with account statements and other important documentation at least once a month. Also, at least for the first several months of the spending plan, household members should continue to maintain records of their miscellaneous cash expenditures.

Hot Tip _____

A good way to help stick to your budget is to label a set of envelopes as rent or mortgage, utilities, car loan, etc. Every month, whenever you get paid, cash your check and put some of that cash in each envelope—enough so that when each bill is due there will be enough cash in the appropriate envelope to pay the bill. Don't touch the cash once you've placed it in the envelope!

If you have a home computer, you may want to invest in a good financial recordkeeping software program. A number of good ones are on the market today. Using such a program can save time, improve your recordkeeping, and enhance your ability to analyze your spending patterns and monitor your progress over time.

Hot Tip _____

Two resources that can help you develop and manage a spending plan are *Quicken* and *The Budget Kit*, CD-ROM and book set. *Quicken* is published by Intuit in both Mac and PC versions. *The Budget Kit*, developed by Judy Lawrence and published by Dearborn Financial Publishing, Inc., can be purchased with a companion CD-ROM for Windows.

ATM machines.   Although having easy access to your bank account 24 hours a day through the use of ATMs is certainly convenient, it can also be very dangerous—especially when you're trying to make a spending plan work. The following tips can help you use ATMs wisely:

- Don't use your ATM card to get money that is not budgeted.
- Establish a specific day of the week to use your ATM card, and before you go to the machine, determine the exact amount of money you will withdraw based on your spending plan. The rest of the week, leave your ATM card at home.

- Leave your ATM card at home when you go shopping or out for the evening. That way, you won't be tempted to get more money after spending your budgeted allotment.
- Save all ATM receipts. Record each withdrawal and deposit in your checkbook register, and make the receipts part of your monthly spending plan records.

Regular meetings.   At the start of each month, everyone in your family should meet to review how well the plan is working, talk over any problems, and make necessary revisions. During these meetings, discuss forthcoming periodic expenses as well as any unanticipated expenses that have arisen, and decide how to adjust your plan so you can pay for them. Once everyone is comfortable with the plan, budget meetings may be necessary only every other month.

To help you determine how well your plan is working, complete a monthly spending plan recap form similar to the one in Figure 2.6. The expense categories listed on the recap form should be identical to those on your spending plan. This form can help you compare what you budgeted to what you actually spent.

Don't get upset if you don't meet your goals right away. Instead, figure out *why* you didn't and how you can do better next time.

As your financial situation changes, your spending plan should be revised. For example, if you've made progress paying off debt or your disposable income has increased, you may want to categorize additional goals as high priority and begin actively working toward them or allocate additional money for the goals you're already working toward.

Teaching Your Children about Money

"The object of education is to prepare the young to educate themselves throughout their lives."

Robert Maynard Hutchins

Developing and living with a spending plan provides you with an ideal opportunity to begin teaching your children how to be smart consumers. By educating them about money and money

---

FIGURE 2.6   Spending Plan Recap: Budgeted versus Actual
Month and Year

	Actual Expenses	*Budgeted Expenses*	*Difference +/–*
Fixed Monthly Expenses			
List your expenses			
Total	$_____	$_____	$_____
Variable Monthly Expenses			
List your expenses			
Total	$_____	$_____	$_____
Periodic Fixed and Variable Monthly Expenses			
List your expenses			
Total	$_____	$_____	$_____
Set Asides			
List your goals			
Total	$_____	$_____	$_____
Total Income	$_____	$_____	$_____
Less Total Expenses	$_____	$_____	$_____
Net Income	$_____		

---

management, you can instill in your children positive lifelong habits that will benefit them as adults. Children as young as three can learn very basic concepts about money, and when a child can count money and understand how to make change, he or she will be ready for a small allowance. Every child is different, so consider your child's abilities and maturity when deciding the best time to begin his or her allowance.

Give the allowance at the same time every week or every month, and make sure your child understands what the allowance is for and that once the money is spent, the child will receive no more until the next allowance date. As your child matures and has more monetary needs, both the size of the allowance and the list of things it can be spent on can increase.

You may want to give your children an opportunity to earn extra money by doing chores around the house. Post a chore sheet in the kitchen, and assign a monetary value to each job. For example, washing the car may be worth $5 and waxing it worth $7. Let your children sign up for any chores they'd like to do. When a task is finished, inspect the work. If it's been done well, pay for the job. If not, explain what needs to be done before you will pay. Doing so will help your children correlate a well-performed chore with money and will help them develop good work habits.

You can also give your children a specific amount of money to spend on holiday or birthday gifts. Use special days as opportunities to teach children comparison shopping—to think about how much they have to spend on a gift before they go shopping and how to look for good buys. This will help them learn to plan ahead, budget their money, and get the most for it. Figure 2. 7 provides ideas for creative gift giving.

Going to a bank with your child and opening your child's first savings account can be a memorable experience. Depositing money in an account, watching it grow, and saving it for something special can help your child understand the concept of interest and the value of saving.

Managing Your Checking Account

"Money is something to make bookkeeping convenient."

H. L. Hunt

Knowing how to reconcile a checkbook is an important money management skill, but surprisingly, it's one many consumers have never learned. If you always had plenty of money and the bank covered your overdrafts, reconciling your checkbook may have seemed like a waste of time. Now, however, if money is tight, it's important that you know exactly how much you have in your checking account. Not knowing can mean costly checking account overdrafts and bad-check charges. They can be devastating when you live on a limited budget.

FIGURE 2.7   Creative Gift Giving and Shopping

Experiment with various types of thoughtful, creative gifts for family and friends. Encourage your children to give gifts of time and talent. Ideas for older children include

- a personalized book of coupons redeemable for special favors—an extra hour of housework, a day's worth of babysitting, a week's worth of taking out the garbage, or a trip to the movies for a younger sibling, for example;
- an album of photos or a scrapbook of memorabilia;
- homemade potpourri or granola stored in an attractive container;
- a handmade ornament or wreath; and
- a framed drawing or photograph.

Check out resale shops when you clothes or toy shop for younger children who are not yet label and status conscious. Also, vintage clothing, used-furniture, antique, and used-book stores can be perfect places to buy gifts for adults who are collectors, have special hobbies, or appreciate the unusual. Don't overlook catalogues. Some offer excellent values, even after shipping and handling costs are factored in.

Hot Tip

Use cash rather than checks as much as possible. Give yourself a weekly cash allowance based on your spending plan to pay for groceries, meals out, gasoline, and other expenses. Keep track of how you're doing as the week progresses. If at the end of the week you have money left over, put it toward one of your goals.

Bouncing a Check

A bounced or returned check is one that your bank can't pay because your account does not have enough money to cover it. This can happen as the result of a number things:

- You forget to record in your check register the checks you write, so you don't maintain a running account balance.
- You make an error in recording in your check register the amount of a check.

- You make an error in calculating your balance.
- You deposit in your account a check that's drawn on a bank other than your own, and you write checks against it before it has had time to clear. When depositing an out-of-town check or a local check drawn on a bank other than your own, ask your bank how long it holds the funds before you can write checks against them.

Your bank charges your account for any check you bounce unless you have overdraft protection. The fee for NSF (not sufficient funds) checks, generally ranging from $5 to $50, is deducted immediately from your account's available balance. In addition, the company to which you wrote the check may charge you a fee, which typically averages about $30, to compensate itself for the loss of income and the cost of collection. If the company to which you wrote the check works with a check recovery firm, you may be required to pay as much as $50 per check. Bouncing a check is obviously a very expensive mistake! When you activate your checking account overdraft protection, you actually borrow money from the bank at a high interest rate. Although it can be a convenient feature, when used carelessly, it can also be dangerous and expensive.

After your bank debits your checking account for the first check you bounce, your account balance may be too low to cover checks you wrote before you realized that your balance was insufficient to cover the first check. Therefore, unless you have increased your checking account balance by depositing more money, these checks will bounce as well, resulting in additional NSF and check recovery charges to your checking account. You may soon find that you have a very serious situation on your hands.

If any of the companies to which you wrote bad checks uses a check approval service, your name and checking account number will now be in the service's computer system, and you'll be unable to write checks to any other business using that same service until you clear up your checks. It is also possible that the businesses to which you wrote bad checks will simply refuse your checks in the future.

Your Checking Account Register

An easy way to avoid problems with your checking account is to record in your check register all transactions as you make them. Record every check you write, noting the amount, name of the payee (the person or company to which the check is written), date, and check number. Also, record and date all of your deposits.

Throughout the month, as you make these entries in your check register, maintain a running account balance by subtracting each check from your previous balance and adding in each deposit. If you use an ATM card, don't forget to adjust your balance accordingly, and do the same for any direct deposits or automatic withdrawals made to your account. This simple routine should help keep you from bouncing checks.

How to Reconcile Your Checkbook

Reconciling your checkbook each month may be a little time consuming, but it is not difficult. Every month, you receive an account statement from your bank detailing the activity in your account for the previous month. This activity includes deposits, cash withdrawals, checks written, and interest earned. The statement itemizes various miscellaneous charges to your account—automatic debits, fees for new checks, bank service charges, insufficient fund charges, ATM transactions, charges to your account for account research done at your request, and so on. It also indicates your ending balance as of the date of the statement, your previous account balance, as well as total deposits, withdrawals, and charges for the period covered by the statement.

Hot Tip

You can save money on the monthly cost of your checking account by ordering checks directly from a check-printing company rather than from your bank. Two such companies are Checks in the Mail (P.O. Box 7802, Irwindale, CA 91706; 800-733-4433) and Current Inc. (Check Printing Department, P.O. Box 19000, Colorado Springs, CO 80935-9000; 800-426-0822). Contact these companies for brochures and pricing information.

When you receive your monthly statement, chronologically organize your canceled checks. Do the same with your deposit slips. Then compare these checks and deposit slips to the entries in your check register, putting a check mark next to each item for which you have a canceled check or deposit slip. Also, make sure that all ATM transactions noted in your bank statement match those recorded in your register.

To have a complete record of all account activities for a given month, record in your checkbook register all account transactions, miscellaneous fees, and charges shown on your statement that are not already noted in your register. Banks do make mistakes, so take note of any transactions you've made that are not reflected in your statement, as well as transactions you didn't make that appear on your statement. If you find something you don't understand, call your bank's customer service office.

Once you have recorded any missing information in your check register and made any necessary corrections, calculate your account balance to arrive at your adjusted checkbook balance. Next, look on the reverse side of your bank statement for the statement reconciliation work area. Figure 2.8 provides a sample reconciliation worksheet. Total all deposits you made after the date of the statement. (They will not show up in your current bank statement, but you should have recorded them in your checkbook.) They are called your deposits outstanding. Write the total for these deposits on the appropriate line of the reconciliation worksheet, then add all the cash withdrawals, checks, ATM charges, and other withdrawals made after the date of your statement. These are your withdrawals outstanding. Record this total on the worksheet line for outstanding checks and charges. On the appropriate line of the worksheet, record the ending balance shown on your current bank statement.

The rest of the reconciliation process is simply a matter of adding and subtracting. Add the ending balance to your total deposits outstanding, and subtract from it your outstanding checks and charges. This dollar figure is your adjusted statement balance and should match the adjusted balance in your checkbook. If it does not, you may have miscalculated, failed to record all account activity, or overlooked a deposit or withdrawal made since the date of your last statement. If you're still having trouble, call or visit your bank's customer service office.

FIGURE 2.8 Sample Reconciliation Worksheet

Reconciliation of Account

Date _____

Please examine this statement and items at once and refer any exceptions immediately by calling us at one of the phone numbers above.

Sort your checks numerically or by date issued.

Mark off in your checkbook each of your checks paid by the bank and list the numbers and amounts of those not paid in the space provided at the left. Include any checks still not paid from previous statements.

Subtract from your checkbook balance any SERVICE CHARGE (S.C.) or bank charge appearing on this statement.

Reconcile your statement in the space provided below.

CHECKS WRITTEN BUT NOT PAID	
NUMBER	AMOUNT

		Enter bank balance from statement			
		Add deposits not credited by bank (if any)			
		TOTAL			
Total of checks not paid		Subtract total of checks not paid			
THIS AMOUNT SHOULD EQUAL YOUR CHECKBOOK BALANCE ➡					

Source: Reprinted by permission of First Valley Bank (203 North Arroyo Blvd., Los Fresnos, Texas).

Hot Tip _____

Don't fall into the trap of not keeping a running balance in your checking account and relying on your overdraft protection. Your bank charges you a high rate of interest for that protection—as much as 22 percent—and it's easy to run up a balance.

Getting the Most for Your Medical Dollars

"I got the bill for my surgery. Now I know what those doctors were wearing masks for."

James H. Boren

The high cost of medical care is no secret these days. It affects everyone. It can eat a substantial chunk of your monthly budget if you're responsible for paying out of your own pocket the cost of enrollment in a fee-for-service insurance plan or a managed care plan, or if you can't afford health care coverage and you have to pay *all* of your medical expenses.

Hot Tip _____

If you lose your job and your former company employs at least 20 workers, the federal Consolidated Omnibus Budget Reconciliation Act (COBRA) gives you the legal right to stay on your employer's health plan for up to 18 months after you work there. However, you must pay the full cost of the insurance—your employer no longer subsidizes it—and that can be expensive.

If you must purchase your own health care coverage, talk to an insurance broker about all of your options. Explain your needs and your financial limitations, and let the agent identify your best, most affordable options. Ordinarily, membership in a managed care organization such as a health maintenance organization (HMO) or preferred provider organization (PPO) is the least expensive choice. However, if you enroll in a traditional fee-for-service health insurance plan, you can decrease the cost of your premium by increasing your deductible. This strategy can make sense if everyone in your family is in good health and rarely needs to see a doctor. But if one of your family members has health problems or takes a lot of medication, a better decision can be to opt for a lower deductible because you'll help minimize your out-of-pocket costs. Also, some insurance carriers will give a discount on your coverage if you pay your premium annually.

Hot Tip ⸻

If you've lost your job and are not covered by COBRA, a short-term option while you evaluate health care coverage possibilities is the purchase of temporary health insurance. It can provide you with catastrophic or major medical health coverage. However, be forewarned—temporary health insurance is expensive.

Once you have health coverage, it's important to know what you can do to control your out-of-pocket medical expenses and maintain an adequate level of health care for your family at the same time. Therefore, the rest of this section provides suggestions for how you can do that. If you're in a managed care plan, many of the suggestions will not apply because you ordinarily have less freedom of choice in managed care than with a fee-for-service insurance plan.

Prescription Drugs

Before your doctor writes your prescription, ask if a generic equivalent is available. You may save up to 50 percent, and you'll suffer no loss in quality. Also, if your doctor understands your financial situation, he or she may be willing to give you some of the free samples of medications pharmaceutical suppliers often give doctors.

With over-the-counter medications, buy the generic or house brands. You can realize significant savings without sacrificing on the effectiveness of the drugs.

Before you get a prescription filled, call drugstores in your area, and shop for the best price. Discount pharmacies often offer substantial savings. If you will take a particular medication for an extended period of time, ask your pharmacist how much you might save by buying in bulk. Some pills or tablets can be split in two. If yours is one of them, buy double the strength, and take only half of the medication. If your pill or tablet doesn't split easily, buy a pill splitter at the drug store.

Mail order pharmacies offer excellent prices on prescription drugs, vitamins, first-aid supplies, and over-the-counter medicines. Request catalogues and prices from Action Mail Order Drug Company, 800-452-1976, Medi-Mail Home Pharmacy, 800-922-3444, and Choice Drug Systems, 800-336-7310. Also, the American Association of Retired Persons (AARP) has a mail order pharmacy for its members, 800-456-2277.

If you're a member of the military or a health professional, you're entitled to discounts when you get your prescriptions filled. Members of other professional associations or special groups may also be eligible for discounts. Ask your pharmacist.

Doctors, Lab Tests, and Other Medical Procedures

Before choosing a general practitioner or medical specialist, call several doctors to see how much they charge for an office visit and to perform certain routine tests and procedures. Assuming their credentials and abilities are equal, select the least expensive. You can check the backgrounds and reputations of doctors by talking to friends or calling your county medical society or local hospital. A doctor with an in-office lab often provides less expensive lab work. This is important because insurance companies frequently pay "usual and customary rates" as averaged over a geographic area. Expensive rates come out of *your* pocket.

Consider seeing a nurse practitioner rather than a doctor for routine problems and gynecological exams. They charge less for their services. Nurse practitioners receive education beyond what registered nurses receive, and they emphasize patient education. If your problem is beyond the ability and training of the nurse practitioner you visit, you will be referred to a doctor. Many nurse practitioners share offices with doctors.

Read up on your medical problem before you see a doctor. Good information will help you ask the right questions and may help you avoid needless and expensive treatments and tests.

Request that your doctor consider your financial limitations when deciding what tests and procedures to order and drugs to prescribe. Before agreeing to any, ask why it is necessary. If you recently had the same tests or procedures performed elsewhere, tell your doctor; it may be possible to get copies of those results. Unless your health is in jeopardy or your doctor needs information to diagnose a problem, postpone all elective medical procedures until they will not seriously strain your budget.

If you feel that your doctor is overprescribing or if you question the necessity of the treatments or diagnostic tests prescribed for you, get a second opinion.

Doctors and labs do make billing mistakes, but the only way you'll know whether your statement is correct—that is, if you got what you paid for—is to get an itemized bill identifying what you received and what it cost.

Hot Tip _____

You can get up-to-date information on 380 medical topics—including various diseases, medical tests and operations, pregnancy, substance abuse, and children's and women's health issues—by calling the Medical Information Line at 900-535-3600. The first 20 seconds of your call are free, and each additional minute thereafter, you are charged a fee. Topics average five minutes in length. The American Academy of Family Physicians reviews the messages for accuracy and completeness.

Hospitals

When you must be hospitalized and you have time to plan ahead, research your options. Comparison shop room rates in your area, and unless your doctor has a convincing reason for you to do otherwise, choose the hospital with the least expensive rates. Avoid hospital admittance and release fees. Call the hospital before you check in to make certain your doctor is not charging you one of these fees. If so, question your doctor about the purpose of such a fee. Check in on a weekday. Unless you are very ill, it makes no sense to check into a hospital on the weekend or late on a Friday—times when most hospitals offer only the most basic services.

Read the hospitalization coverage information provided by your insurance company or managed care plan. Be aware of what you can do to decrease your costs and what you should avoid doing so you don't increase your costs.

After your hospitalization, review your hospital bill carefully to make sure that you are charged for services you actually used and medications you took. If you are confused by your bill, ask questions, and do not pay for anything you did not receive.

Shopping at Pawnshops

For many people, the word *pawnshop* probably brings to mind a dark, slightly disreputable store patronized by unsavory individuals. While this type of pawnshop still exists, certain segments of the pawnshop industry have spent a considerable amount of money to change that image to attract a more up-scale clientele. These pawnshops are now attractive places to shop and feature service-oriented salespeople.

Pawnshops can offer excellent bargains on a variety of merchandise, including tools, cameras, bicycles, and electronic items. To get the best deals possible, here are some basic rules for pawnshop shopping:

- Negotiate on price. Often an item's marked price is not the lowest price the shop will take. Try bargaining.
- Before you go to a pawnshop to buy a specific item, know how much you would pay if you bought the item new at a discount retailer in your area.
- Comparison shop. The variety, quality, and price of merchandise vary from pawnshop to pawnshop, so visit several to see which offers the best deal.
- Make sure the item you consider buying works to your satisfaction and that it's not an obsolete or a discontinued item that will be difficult to find parts for or to repair.
- Before you purchase anything, especially a big-ticket item, ask about the store's return and guarantee policies. No deal is a good deal if what you buy turns out to be defective and you're stuck with it. Some pawnshops will not guarantee their merchandise once you leave with it; others will guarantee the working condition of the merchandise and take it back if it fails to live up to your expectations.

Travel on a Shoestring Budget

When money is tight, traveling can be a challenge, but it's not impossible. Plan your travel ahead of time so you can revise your spending plan to accommodate your travel expenses and so that you can take advantage of any discounts that may be available if you book your hotel and plane reservations early.

This section provides information and tips for traveling on a shoestring budget. It also provides advice for those who may not have access to credit cards for guaranteeing hotel reservations or for reserving a rental car.

Hotels and Motels

If you are a business traveler and know where your meetings will be, try to find a hotel close to them so you won't have to rent a car or pay for cabs. Then, well in advance of the date you plan to travel, call the 800 number of the hotel or motel you will stay at to make your reservation. (To get this number, call 800 directory assistance—800-555-1212.)

Hot Tip _____

Prepaying your hotel stay allows you to travel without having to carry a lot of cash. When you do need large amounts of cash, always use traveler's checks.

Most hotels expect travelers to guarantee their reservations with credit cards. If you don't have a major national bankcard, ask the reservation clerk about the hotel's "creditless" travel policy. Some hotel chains have companywide creditless policies; others allow each hotel in their chains to set its own policy. Following are descriptions of what some major hotels and motels require of creditless travel.

Marriott. With one exception, this chain allows each of its hotels to set its own policy for creditless travelers. (At Marriott's resort hotels, you must guarantee your room with a credit card, no exceptions.) Generally, if you want to guarantee a room for late arrival—after 6 PM—you must send a check or money order for the first night's stay, seven to ten days after you make your reservation, or up to 30 days before your arrival. Some Marriotts make late arrival reservations without a deposit by accepting a corporate or company guarantee of payment. For more information, call 800-228-9290.

Hilton.   Hilton hotels accept a company or personal check for the first night's stay. The check must be received seven to ten days after you make your reservation. In many cases, you can also make arrangements for prepayment of your entire stay, although you should ask the hotel's credit manager for its specific policy. For more information, call 800-445-8667.

Hyatt.   Each Hyatt hotel has its own policy, but some guarantee to a traveler's home address until a deposit for the first night has been received. Company and personal checks are accepted. At some hotels, travelers who are members of Hyatt's Gold Passport Program may have to guarantee their reservations with credit cards or deposits. For more information, call 800-233-1234.

Holiday Inn.   Each Holiday Inn sets its own policies. Some hotels allow you to guarantee your room for late arrival by mailing a money order for one night's stay; others accept credit only. However, you can guarantee your room with your account number if the company you work for has a corporate account with Holiday Inn. For details on a corporate account, call 800-343-5545; if you live in Massachusetts, call 800-792-5163. For more information on Holiday Inn's policies for travelers not using credit, call 800-465-4329.

Motel 6.   You can either prepay with cash at the Motel 6 closest to you for a stay at the Motel 6 location you will use during your travels, or you can send a personal check to the motels where you'll stay. You must send your check at least 14 days before arrival. Motel 6 does not accept personal or company checks at the time of check-in or check-out. For more information, call 800-466-8356.

Choice Hotels International.   (Choice Hotels, Clarion Hotels, Quality Inn, Comfort Inn, Sleep Inn, Rodeway Inn, Econolodge, and Friendship Inn.) Each hotel in the Choice chain has its own policy regarding creditless travelers. In general, however, a traveler must get the room deposit to the hotel by the day of arrival if the traveler pays with a money order, and ten days before arrival if the traveler uses a personal check. No personal or company checks are accepted at the time of check-in or check-out. A traveler can also go to any hotel in the chain ahead of time, pay a deposit for the first night's hotel stay, and get a voucher for late check-in. For information, call 800-221-2222.

Hotel and Motel Discounts

Many hotels and motels offer substantial discounts on their rooms—weekend packages and off-season rates, for example. To learn about discounts, call a hotel directly, and ask what packages and special rates it offers. Discount information is *not* information that will be volunteered when you make your reservation. Some hotels, like Marriott and Days Inn, give discounts for reserving rooms well in advance, so ask what's available.

An important drawback of early reservation discount programs is that you usually must pay a penalty if you cancel your reservation. Therefore, when you get information about discounts, be sure to find out about the hotel's cancellation policy.

If you travel frequently and tend to stay at the same hotel or at hotels in the same chain, find out whether the hotels have frequent-stay programs you can enroll in. You may be able to build up credits toward a free room or other freebies or discounts. Also, request a corporate rate when making reservations. This usually gets you a 10 percent discount.

If you're a senior citizen, you may be eligible for a senior discount. Ask at the time you make your reservation if the hotel offers such a discount. As a member of the American Association of Retired Persons (AARP), you can get discounts of up to 30 percent at many hotels. For membership information, call 202-434-2277.

Other professional or association memberships may entitle you to discounts on your accommodations. Call your association headquarters to find out about the benefits of membership.

Hot Tip

Never wait for a hotel reservation clerk to tell you about discounts that may be available. Usually, the clerk won't tell you unless you ask.

FIGURE 2.9   Sources for Discount Hotel Accommodations

- *Travel America at Half Price,* Entertainment Publications. This publication lists 1,200 hotels and motels and costs $36. To order, call 800-342-0558.
- International Travel Card Program. As a member, one of your benefits is a copy of *Hotels at Half Price.* Membership is $36 per year. To find out about joining, call 800-342-0558.
- Concierge Club. Membership in this club, which specializes in up-scale hotels, costs $49.95 per year. To find out about membership, call 800-952-9537.

Other tips for getting discounted hotel and motel rooms follow:

- Join a half-price hotel club. For a modest fee, you get a directory of hotels and motels that give discounts of up to 50 percent on the regular rate for a standard room. Figure 2.9 tells how to get information about some of these clubs as well as other sources of discount hotel accommodations.
- Use the services of a discount booking service when making reservations at a hotel or motel. Depending on the service, you can get discounts of up to 65 percent off standard rates. However, you may have to pay the full amount of your stay up front. Figure 2.10 provides telephone numbers for some discount hotel-booking services.
- Suggest a company subscription to *Frequent Flyer,* a publication reporting on frequent-stay and frequent-flyer programs and other travel information. For subscription information, write to 1775 Broadway, 19th Floor, New York, New York 10019; or call 212-237-3000.

Rental Cars

If you need a rental car while you travel, advance planning allows you to take advantage of any discounts or packages. If you don't have a national bankcard, advance planning is essential. Following are the requirements of several major rental car companies for renting a car without using credit.

FIGURE 2.10   Discount Hotel-Booking Services

- ·Washington, D.C. Accommodations—800-503-3338. Washington, D.C. 20 percent to 60 percent discount.
- Express Hotel Reservations—800-356-1123. New York City and Los Angeles. 20 percent to 40 percent discount.
- Central Reservation Service—800-548-3311. Boston, Los Angeles, New York City, Orlando, Miami, and San Francisco. 20 percent discount.
- Room Exchange—800-846-7000. 900 cities across the United States as well as cities in Europe, Asia, and the Caribbean. 20 percent to 50 percent discount.

Avis.   Avis offers creditless travelers two options. The first is to pay with cash. To do so, you must complete an application and provide bank, personal, and employment references. In addition, Avis wants proof that you're employed and have been with your company for at least one year; that you are at least 25 years old; that you have a phone listed in your name; and that your phone number and address are in your local directory under your name. If you pay with cash, you must leave a deposit of between $200 and $300 or 30 percent of the total estimated rental cost—whichever is greater—at the time of rental, and your rental fee comes out of this deposit.

The second option available through Avis requires that your company establish a corporate account. As an employee, you would be an authorized rep, and the rental bill would go to your employer. For more information, call 800-331-1212.

Hertz.   If you're at least 25 years old, Hertz will let you apply for a special card that substitutes for a credit card. To apply, you must complete an Advanced Cash Qualification Application and pay a nonrefundable $15 application fee. This $15 covers the cost of checking your credit history. If you're approved for the card, whenever you use it to rent a car, you must pay the estimated costs of the rental plus a 50 percent surcharge. When you return the car, you must pay the balance due, if any, with cash, a personal or corporate check, or a money order. For more information, call 202-307-2000.

Thrifty.   Some locations accept credit cards only. Others allow travelers to cash qualify. A request to cash qualify must be directed in advance to the particular rental location you will use. The specific terms and conditions of rental without a credit card vary from location to location. For more information, call 800-367-2277.

DOLLAR Rent-A-Car.   Every rental location has its own policy, so call ahead to the location you use. Some locations do not accept cash, while others accept cash, but also want a $500 to $1,500 deposit. Some locations rent to drivers between the ages of 21 and 24 for an additional fee. For more information, call 800-327-7607.

Additional Travel Tips

Here are some more tips for traveling on a budget:

- Because hotel food prices tend to be high, if possible, select a hotel close to well-priced restaurants and to restaurants that don't rely primarily on travelers and tourists for their business. Well-priced restaurants don't have to mean fast-food; they can also be ethnic restaurants, delis, and places frequented by the locals. Dining in local eateries, not hotel restaurants, will save you money and also give you a sense of the culture and regional uniqueness of the city you visit. Find out about some of these restaurants by reading local travel guides and city publications. The chamber of commerce in the city you visit may be a resource as well.
- Pack tins of food together with crackers and cheese. If your stay will not be lengthy, you can actually have a gourmet suitcase feast for a lot less than it would cost to eat out!
- Use public transportation as much as possible.

Consumer Telemarketing Scams

"Let every eye negotiate for itself, and trust no agent."
William Shakespeare

When you struggle to make ends meet, the sales pitch of a telemarketer claiming that he or she has a great deal for you can be very tempting. You need to be careful, however, because telemarketers often peddle consumer scams. In fact, according to the Federal Trade Commission (FTC), consumers lose more than $40 billion a year to telemarketing fraud. These companies sell anything and everything—from investment opportunities to Bahama cruises. To gain your confidence, telemarketers frequently act overly friendly and will seem to know a lot about you. Many use high-pressure sales tactics to get you to buy what they sell, and they provide little information about the investments, services, or products they're offering.

Although it's impossible to list every existing scam or anticipate those to come, this chapter highlights the most common consumer scams—those conducted by fraudulent telemarketers—and discusses how to recognize them.

Common Consumer Scams

Here are some examples of products, services, and "opportunities" that are usually scams:

Partially developed or undeveloped land.   You'll be told what a wonderful deal you're being offered, how fast the land is selling, and that prices will start rising soon.

Travel packages.   Often, you will learn about a bogus travel package by mail and will be referred to a 900 number for more details. On the surface, the package may sound legitimate and attractive. But when you call the 900 number, you'll find out that there's a catch—for example, you need to pay a fee to join a travel club to take advantage of the offer. Many of the people who respond to these ads never get their free trips or discount travel packages because their reservations are not confirmed or because the conditions of travel are too restrictive or too expensive.

Some travel scams don't require that you do anything special to take advantage of an offer. However, when you take the trip, the accommodations are nothing like their description in the brochures and other information you received, and they are not worth even the low price you paid for your trip.

Advance-fee loans and credit.   You'll be promised a loan or a credit card even if you have bad credit, but you'll have to pay a fee in advance, as much as several hundred dollars. What you may end up with for your money is a list of banks, finance companies, and other financial institutions to which you can apply for credit.

Investments.   Offers to buy gems, oil and gas leases, coins, precious metals, and interests in oil wells are scams disguised as investment opportunities. You may be notified by phone that you've been selected to participate in a fantastic investment opportunity and asked to send money right away.

Magazines.   Some companies try to trick consumers into purchasing multiple-year subscriptions to magazines they could buy more cheaply through another source or don't really want in the first place. Initially, you may be led to believe that you've won a sweepstakes or a prize, but the conversation will soon switch to magazine subscriptions.

Gold cards.   Marketers of gold or platinum cards imply in their advertising that you can get major national bankcards after using the marketers' cards and that their cards can help you improve your credit record. Rarely is this true. Consumers who get a gold or platinum card usually can use it only to order a limited array of merchandise from a catalogue provided by the marketer—and the consumers may have to pay an additional fee to order from the catalogue. Additionally, consumers who apply for one of these cards are often charged a substantial application or initiation fee.

How Telemarketers Work

Fraudulent telemarketers usually contact you in one of three ways:

1. By phone.   The caller will have gotten your name from either a mailing list or the phone book. When a mailing list is the source, the caller often uses a lot of personal information about you in an attempt to build trust and credibility.

2. A letter or postcard.   This mail often tells you that you have won a prize or a trip and that to collect it, you must send something back through the mail, provide certain information, or make a phone call. If you do, a salesperson will call you and use a persuasive sales pitch, scare tactics, or exaggerated claims to deceive you and get your money.

FIGURE 2.11   General Tips for Protecting Yourself from Telemarketing Scams

- Ask for written information about any offer. Review it carefully.
- Don't pay any money up front or sign any paperwork before you know an offer is legitimate.
- Don't send any money by courier, overnight delivery, or wire to anyone who insists on immediate payment.
- Physically inspect any property or merchandise before you buy it.
- Hang up on high-pressure telemarketers.
- Take your time to evaluate any offer; don't be pressured into making your decision on the phone.
- Don't give your credit card number, bank account number, or any other financial information to anyone who tries to sell you something over the phone.
- Check out any telemarketer with your state attorney general's office or state office of consumer protection as well as your local Better Business Bureau before you do business with it.

---

3. TV and print ads.   Some telemarketing companies use advertising to entice consumers to call a phone number—often a costly 900 number—for additional information or to complete an application.

If You're Victimized by a Telemarketing Scam

When talking to a telemarketer, keep in mind the tips offered in Figure 2.11. Following these tips will help protect you from getting ripped off by a bogus sales pitch. In addition, you should know about the important protections the FTC's new Telemarketing Sales Rule offers you. Here are some of its provisions:

- It's illegal for a telemarketer to continue calling if you say you don't want to be contacted.
- Telemarketers may call only between 8 AM and 9 PM.
- You must be told at the start of a telemarketer's call that it's a sales call.
- If a telemarketer calls you about a prize promotion, the salesperson must tell you the odds that you'll win and that you don't need to buy or pay anything to win.

- It's illegal for a telemarketer to mislead you in any way.
- You must be told the total cost of the product or service a telemarketer tries to sell you and any restrictions and conditions of purchase.
- You do not have to pay in advance for any credit repair, recovery room, or advance-fee loan or credit services. (Credit repair firms are discussed in Chapter 8.) Recovery room salespeople call consumers who have been ripped off by telemarketers and promise that for a fee or a donation to a certain charity, they can get the consumers' money back or get the prizes or products they were promised and never received.

If a telemarketer violates any of these rules, contact your state attorney general's office or state consumer protection office. The Telemarketing Sales Rule gives these state offices enforcement powers. You may also want to file a complaint with the FTC at Correspondence Branch, Washington, DC 20580.

Hot Tip _____

Contact the National Fraud Information Center about instances of telemarketing fraud by calling 800-876-7060. This private, nonprofit organization operates a hot line to provide services and assistance to consumers. It also reports all complaints to the FTC's telemarketing fraud database.

What You Should Know before Calling a 900 Telephone Number

Many companies and organizations make legitimate use of 900 numbers by indicating up front what the charge will be for a call and explaining exactly what you will get if you make the call. (Unlike an 800 number, when you call a 900 number, you are charged a flat fee or a per-minute fee for the call.) However, fraudulent telemarketers often charge excessively for 900 calls or fail to give you what they led you to expect you would receive.

To avoid being victimized by a 900 scam, here are some things you should do:

- Know exactly how much the call will cost before you make it. This cost should be stated up front.
- Deal only with companies you are familiar with or that you know have good reputations. Many reputable firms use 900 numbers to conduct surveys or provide useful consumer information.
- Avoid making 900-number calls to order free gifts or prizes because you'll pay for them with your calls.
- Tell your children how 900 numbers work, and ask them not to call a 900 number without your permission.
- Check each phone bill to make sure it does not contain charges for 900-number calls.

Figure 2.12 also provides tips for spotting a 900-number telephone scam.

Hot Tip _____

Local 976 and long-distance 700 exchanges are often used like 900 numbers. Follow the same advice and warnings with these two exchanges.

If You're a Victim

If you are victimized by a 900-number scam, contact your telephone company, and ask that any charges be deleted from your bill. Although phone companies are not obligated to do so, many will delete the charges as a gesture of goodwill.

Another option is to ask the phone company to give you the name and address of the company that charged you for the 900-number call. Write that company, and request that it delete the charge. If it doesn't and you refuse to pay, you risk having your account turned over to a debt collector and negatively affecting your credit record. At this point, follow the advice in Chapter 6 for dealing with debt collectors and in Chapter 7 about your credit record.

If you have a problem with a 900 number or with any other type of phone scam, contact the office of your state attorney general or the office of consumer affairs, as well as the FTC.

FIGURE 2.12   How to Recognize a 900-Number Scam

- You aren't told how much the call will cost.
- You are told the per-minute rate, but not the number of minutes you will be on the line.
- The recorded message you hear when you call the 900 number runs so quickly that you have to call back several times to understand it all.
- The company is vague about what you'll get if you call or makes grandiose promises about the information, product, or service you'll receive.

Blues Busters

Living paycheck to paycheck doesn't have to mean an end to fun and pleasure. You can still have a good life even if you don't have a lot of money for extras. However, to make the most of your money, you need sound money management skills, you need to know how to get bargains on food and merchandise, and you need to be able to spot bogus telemarketers. This chapter should have served as a good introduction to some of this basic information.

THREE

Making More Money

> "I don't have anything against work. I just figure why deprive somebody who really loves it?"
>
> **Dobie Gillis**

Karla S. had a job that offered her few opportunities for advancement. Recently divorced, she knew it was up to her to provide for herself and her 12-year-old son. Her ex-husband sent irregular child support payments—nothing she could count on.

To give herself and her son the kinds of opportunities she wanted, Karla decided to return to school to become a nurse. But that meant she had to find a way to make more money so she could finance her education.

Although Karla was smart and highly motivated, she had no idea how to find a better-paying job. Therefore, at the suggestion of a friend whom I had worked with, Karla made an appointment with me so we could discuss how she might accomplish her goals and so I could tell her what resources were available to help her. I gave her copies of listings for jobs available through her city and state governments and told her about other sources of employment information she might use to identify opportunities for earning extra money. We also talked about possible sources of financial aid for nursing school and what Karla might do right away to help ensure academic success (she was concerned about her math skills). In addition, I told her about the free career counseling services sponsored by a local women's center, encouraged her to look into a program offered by a nearby community college for working women who wanted to go back to school, and gave her information about some federal educational assistance programs. Karla left my office with a smile on her face. Although she realized that achieving her goals would take time and hard work, she now also knew the resources that could help her.

You may need extra money for many reasons. Here are just a few:

- You've lost your regular job and have some money saved, but while you look for a new one, you want extra money to help pay the bills so you don't use up your savings.
- Although your former employer gave you a good severance package, with your current obligations, the money will not last long.
- You've accepted a new full-time job at a salary that is a lot less than what you used to make, and you're having a hard time making ends meet.
- You want to go back to school to update your job skills or to acquire new skills.
- You've decided to start your own business or to work as an independent contractor, and you need extra cash to help get you through the start-up years, when money is tight.
- You want to pay off your debt or build up your savings.

Whatever your reasons for wanting to earn more money, this chapter will give you some ideas for doing that.

Know Your Options

You have many ways to make more money. They include working overtime, finding a better-paying job, and taking a second job, or moonlighting. If you decide to moonlight, you'll become part of a growing trend among both highly skilled professionals and blue-collar workers. According to the Bureau of Labor Statistics, in 1995, about 8 million people, or 6.4 percent of all American workers, held second jobs—the highest percentage in more than 30 years. Starting a part-time business is another option.

Hot Tip

According to many career counselors, constantly upgrading and increasing your job skills and credentials is key to remaining marketable in today's job world. The more you can offer an employer, the more valuable you are as an employee and the more options you have, whether you want to continue working for someone else or want to become self-employed.

Furthering your education or developing new job skills may be a prerequisite to earning more money. For example, technology may have diminished the market value of your current skills, or success in the new career you want to pursue or the business you want to begin may require additional education or training.

Hot Tip

Don't be reluctant to work at a job that you think is beneath you or because the pay is low. When you need to make more money, it may be time to swallow your pride. Minimum wage is better than no wage!

How to Find a Better-Paying Job

"If you only knock long enough and loud enough at the gate, you are sure to wake up somebody."
Henry Wadsworth Longfellow

Making more money may be a matter of finding a better-paying job in your current profession. If you already have good skills and a solid résumé and you live in an area where job opportunities abound, finding new employment may be relatively easy. However, whatever your situation, if you're employed, don't quit your current job until you have a new one.

Following are some suggestions for finding a new job:

- Tell close friends, family members, and professional acquaintances that you're in the job market, and ask them to keep their eyes and ears open for any opportunities they think might be of interest to you. As you're probably aware, many jobs are never advertised in the newspaper classifieds, but are filled through word of mouth.
- Ask your professional associates and coworkers whether they can suggest people you should meet with—not to talk about specific jobs, but to brainstorm about possible job leads.
- Read the employment ads in the classifieds section of your local newspaper and in the newspapers of towns and cities within commuting distance. The professional newsletters and trade publications you subscribe to may also run job ads.
- Track companies moving into your area. They may be looking for people with your job skills and experience. Your local chamber of commerce can be an information source, as can your state's commerce department or office of economic development.
- Contact each company you'd like to work for even if it doesn't have a job opening in your area of expertise. Fill out a job application, or send a résumé to the head of the division or department you'd like placement in. Attach a cover letter to your résumé expressing your interest in being considered for an appropriate position should one open up. Follow with a phone call.
- Your union or professional association may maintain a job bank or provide other types of job-finding assistance. Take advantage of these resources.
- If you're a relatively high-paid professional, schedule appointments with executive recruitment or executive search firms. Before you do, be certain you have a well-prepared, up-to-date résumé. See Figure 3.1 for résumé preparation hints. If you need more help, visit your local library for books and magazine articles about preparing a résumé that sells, or get help from a firm that specializes in preparing résumés.

FIGURE 3.1   Preparing a Résumé

Résumés follow no set format. However, when preparing a résumé, remember the following:

- Keep it as brief as possible, but long enough to clearly convey the breadth and depth of your experience.
- Avoid misspellings and grammatical errors.
- For a professional look, print your résumé on neutral-colored paper.
- Avoid gimmicks.
- Either attach a separate sheet listing the names, titles, addresses, and phone numbers of your references, or indicate "references available upon request" at the bottom of your résumé.
- Include this standard information in your résumé:
  - Your name, address, and telephone number.
  - Your employment history. For each position listed, identify your employer's name and address, note the dates you held that position, and describe your responsibilities and accomplishments.
- Note your educational background, including your degrees, the schools you attended, graduation dates, majors, and special awards and recognitions.
- List special skills, achievements, professional or civic organization memberships, awards, and other noteworthy information.

- Attend local job fairs. They can be good ways to learn about companies that are hiring and the types of employees they're looking for. Company representatives are usually on hand to answer your questions and maybe even to conduct an initial interview.
- Attend professional networking breakfasts, luncheons, or happy hours. These events can be good sources of job leads.
- Contact your local or county human resources or personnel department to learn about its job placement and referral services.
- Call the Federal Job Information Center about federal government employment opportunities (800-688-9889).
- Schedule appointments with several of the larger job placement or personnel agencies listed in your local Yellow Pages under Employment or Jobs. Although they may not

---

FIGURE 3.2   Three Tips for Getting the Job Help You Need

1. Work with a company that regularly fills the type of position you're looking for or that specializes in placing people with your salary requirements. Be clear about who will pay the company's fee. If you have to pay, find out how the fee is determined, when the fee is due, and whether you must pay the fee even if the company doesn't place you in a job.
2. Before you sign an agreement with an employment assistance company, read it carefully, and question anything you do not understand.
3. Depending on the kind of position you're looking for, review employment ads in trade and professional publications, talk with your own professional contacts, attend networking events, and read your newspaper's classified employment ads to identify job leads and the right employers to contact.

---

have a position that is right for you when you meet with them, if you impress them with your attitude, skills, and experience, they may call you later when they have something appropriate for you.

- Visit or call your state's job service or public employment service. These offices maintain information about job vacancies in the government sector and may also have information on private-sector and nonprofit organization jobs. In addition, they may be able to provide you with job counseling and referral services, job search training, résumé development assistance, and skills assessment services. Many of these services are specifically targeted toward laid-off workers; veterans are always given priority treatment.

Outside Help

If you want help finding a job, familiarize yourself with the various types of companies and organizations that offer job-finding assistance so you can select the one most appropriate for you. Some of these resources may also be able to help you improve your interviewing skills and your résumé, or can tell you where such help is available.

Figure 3.2 provides tips on getting help finding a job, and Figure 3.3 provides advice on job interviews.

FIGURE 3.3   How to Have a Good Job Interview

- Research a potential employer before your job interview. Learn as much as you can about its history and successes, its products or services, its long-term and short-term goals, and any challenges it faces. To get this information, talk to friends or acquaintances who work there; read its annual report; and do an information search at the library. If it's a large national or regional employer, there may be articles about it in newspapers and magazines. Also, search the Internet for information. Familiarize yourself with the kinds of challenges businesses or organizations like it face in general. Also, learn as much as you can about the person who will interview you.
- Spend time assessing your strengths (and weaknesses) and special accomplishments. Think in terms of what you can contribute to a potential employer.
- Role play. Get a friend or professional associate to ask you questions you might face during an interview so you can decide how best to phrase your answers.
- Act confident, but don't dominate the interview.
- Don't ask about salary, vacation time, sick leave, or other perquisites. These are appropriate subjects during a follow-up interview or if you are offered the job.
- Look directly at the interviewer when you talk and pay close attention when the interviewer speaks.

Hot Tip

Before you sign an agreement with or pay any money to a company offering to help you find a temporary or permanent job, understand exactly how the company can help you, the costs involved, and whether you or the potential employer will pay those costs.

The following paragraphs discuss the main sources of employment assistance.

Employment agencies and personnel placement services. These firms help companies fill specific job vacancies. Sometimes, the hiring company pays a placement fee to the employ-

---

FIGURE 3.4   How to Protect Yourself from Job Scams

- Don't call an employment ad with a 900 number.
- Avoid companies that advertise jobs, but require money upfront before they will tell you about any of them.
- Ask for information in writing before you work with a company that advertises jobs.
- If you're unsure about a job opportunity or the company advertising it, contact your state attorney general's office or state office of consumer affairs and the better business bureau in your town as well as the town where the company is located to find out whether any complaints have been lodged against it.

---

ment agency; other times, the fee is shared by the employer and the new employee; and sometimes it's paid entirely by the new employee.

Executive search firms or executive recruiters.   Search firms, often referred to as headhunters, are often used by businesses as well as nonprofit organizations to help them fill relatively high-salaried positions. The company doing the hiring pays all of the executive search firm's fees.

Hot Tip _____

Steer clear of job scams. The companies advertising these scams may use the mail, TV or radio, or phone calls to tell you about the "guaranteed" jobs they offer and the fantastic money you will earn. Anything that sounds too good to be true usually is. See Figure 3.4 for tips on protecting yourself from job scams.

Temporary agencies.   These agencies place skilled and unskilled workers in temporary positions that can last for just a few days to months. A growing number of independent contractors find work through temporary agencies. Usually, the employer pays the agency's fees.

Public employment service or job service offices.   Operated across the country, these publicly funded offices are sources of free job information. They are federally mandated to provide special assistance to Vietnam veterans, laid-off workers, welfare recipients, the handicapped, older workers, youths, and minorities.

Changing Careers

"If at first you don't succeed, you are running about average."
                                                    M. H. Anderson

Changing careers is a big but sometimes necessary step when you need to make more money. Your employer may have gone out of business or dramatically reduced its permanent workforce—including you—and few if any opportunities may exist in your area for someone with your skills and experience. Or the demand for your job skills may be dwindling due to a changing economy or new technology, and you can no longer command the salary you once could.

You can use a number of helpful resources to learn about the occupations for which a growing or a declining demand exists. For example, the Department of Labor's Bureau of Labor Statistics (BLS) publishes excellent free brochures that provide job growth and salary information for a variety of industries and occupations, general information about the kinds of education and training they require, and helpful job-finding advice. For a complete list of these publications and for cost information, call 312-353-1880, or go to the BLS web site at http://stats.bls.gov/emphome.htm.

See Figure 3.5. for the outlook on some selected occupations between 1994 and 2005.

Hot Tip ⎯⎯⎯⎯⎯⎯⎯⎯⎯⎯⎯⎯⎯⎯⎯⎯⎯⎯⎯

When you look for a new career, focus on one that will allow you to develop a wide variety of skills that you could use in several work settings and that are projected to be in demand over the coming years. Maximize your options.

FIGURE 3.5   Outlook for Selected Occupations

Occupations projected for fast rates of growth between 1994 and 2005 include the following (small sampling of the jobs listed by BLS):

Jobs Requiring a Professional or an Advanced Degree

Chiropractor
College or university professor
Counselor
Lawyer
Management analyst
Medical or biological scientist
Podiatrist

Jobs Requiring Work Experience Plus a Bachelor's Degree

Artist or commercial artist
Education administrator
Financial manager
Marketing, advertising, or public relations manager

Jobs Requiring a Bachelor's Degree

Computer engineer
Occupational or physical therapist
Special education teacher
Systems analyst

Jobs Requiring an Associate Degree

Dental hygienist
Medical records technician
Paralegal
Respiratory therapist

Jobs Requiring Postsecondary Vocational Training

Data processing equipment repairer
Emergency medical technician
Manicurist
Surgical technologist

FIGURE 3.5   Outlook for Selected Occupations   (Continued)

Jobs Requiring Work Experience or On-the-Job Training

Clerical supervisor or manager
Corrections officer
Food service or lodging manager
Human services worker
Lawn service manager
Medical assistant
Nursery or greenhouse manager
Personal or home health care aide
Securities or financial services salesperson

Source: Information taken from *Tomorrow's Jobs*, U.S. Department of Labor, Bureau of Labor Statistics, February 1996.

Hot Tip ————————————

For an in-depth analysis of the training, skills, and knowledge necessary for selecting and developing a successful new career in the '90s, read *The 100 Best Jobs for the 1990s & Beyond*, Dearborn Financial Publishing, Inc., 1992. Written by Carol Kleiman, one of the nation's foremost authorities on jobs and the workplace, this book includes information on the fastest-growing job fields, inside tips on finding a job, and advice on changing jobs and preparing for the future.

One of the best ways to learn about new career possibilities is to talk with people already working in professions or industries that interest you. They can tell you about the education and training you need, discuss available opportunities, describe typical workdays and what they like most and least about their jobs, provide you with overviews of wages or salaries (starting and potential) in their professions, and discuss advancement opportunities and future outlooks for their occupations.

FIGURE 3.6   Sources of Career and Job-Hunting Information

The Department of Labor publishes a number of useful publications, including the following:

- *Occupational Outlook Handbook, 1996–1997 Edition*
- *Tomorrow's Jobs*
- *Résumés, Application Forms, Cover Letters, and Interviews*
- *Getting Back to Work*
- *Tips for Finding the Right Job*

All of these publications are available free of charge or for a nominal fee. You can order the first two through the Bureau of Labor Statistics' Publications Sales Center at P.O. Box 2145, Chicago, IL 60690, or call 312-353-1880. To order the second two publications, write to the *Consumer Information Catalog,* Consumer Information Center, P.O. Box 100, Pueblo, CO 81002.

Tips for Finding the Right Job provides advice about writing résumés, interviewing, and taking preemployment tests. You can find this book at most state-run Public Employment Service offices, or order it by calling 202-512-1800. It costs $1.25.

Other sources of career information include public employment offices, federally funded job-training programs, and companies in the business of providing career counseling. Some of these firms will use testing and other techniques to help you figure out what you'd like to do and what you'd be best at. See Figure 3.6 for additional sources of career and job-hunting information.

Hot Tip

To help you analyze your strengths and weaknesses so you can figure out the kind of jobs you're best suited for, read the most recent edition of *What Color Is Your Parachute?* by Richard Nelson Bolles, Ten Speed Press, 1996.

Job Training and Career Education

"There will never be a system invented that will do away with the necessity of work."

Henry Ford

Depending on your career choice, attending a private trade or technical school can be a good way to learn new job skills. Remember, though, these schools are in business to make a profit, and although many provide excellent value for the money, others put making money ahead of providing quality education. Some less reputable schools use high-pressure sales tactics and unrealistic promises of great salaries and glamorous work after graduation to get students to enroll. Many charge exorbitant prices for providing students with skills and knowledge that have little real market value or that the students could have acquired at far less cost by attending a community college.

Hot Tip

If you borrowed federal funds to help pay for the costs of a trade or technical school, and you believe that the school did not provide the education it promised or overpromised the career possibilities you would enjoy upon graduation, or if the school won't refund your tuition as per your agreement, contact the U.S. Department of Education at 800-647-8733. In Washington, D.C., call 755-2770.

Selecting a Trade or Technical School

To avoid becoming a trade or technical school victim, use the following guidelines to help you select a reputable school:

- Avoid schools that try to pressure you into enrolling. Many "admissions counselors" are no more than salespeople who earn a commission every time they sign up a new student.
- Ask for printed information describing a school's programs and costs, including tuition, lab fees, equipment, uniforms, books, other classroom materials, and meals. Also, request general background information on a school's history and credentials. Steer clear of schools that don't have printed information or won't give clear answers to your questions.

- Visit any school you consider, and ask to see its class-rooms, labs, and other teaching-related facilities.
- Ask to sit in on one or more of the classes you would take if you enrolled.
- If possible, talk to students currently attending the school you're considering to learn whether they're satisfied with the training and education they receive. Also, ask the school for the names and phone numbers of several gradu-ates of the program you're interested in so you can talk with them about how readily they found jobs at the salaries they wanted after graduation.
- Talk to administrators or counselors about a school's aca-demic standards and the criteria used to select students.
- Contact some of the employers you'd like to work for after you finish your education, and ask them to evaluate the curriculum you would be studying. Find out whether they would be more apt to hire you if you completed the program.
- Be wary of any school that does not straightforwardly explain the pros and cons of the financial aid you might receive or that fails to convey to you that a student loan is just that—a loan you must repay.
- Find out what a school's student loan default rate is by call-ing 800-688-9889.
- Find out about the background and experience of the teachers in a program. Do they have the appropriate cre-dentials and skills?
- If you will be trained to use special equipment, make sure that it's state of the art. Also, make sure that the school has enough equipment that all students in your program will have sufficient opportunities to use it.
- Compare the program and costs of any school you con-sider with those of community colleges and adult educa-tion programs in your area to find the best value.
- Find out about a school's job placement program and its job placement rates.
- Avoid a school if its administrators are evasive, act secre-tive, or make grandiose promises that they won't put in writing.
- Ask what organizations have licensed and accredited a school.

- Call your area's better business bureau and the office of your state attorney general or your state's consumer protection office to find out whether any complaints against a school have been registered.

A College Education

You may decide to get an undergraduate or a graduate degree as a way of increasing your earnings power. If you're lucky, you live within commuting distance of a community college or private institution. Many of these schools offer classes at night to accommodate the growing number of students who combine education with full-time jobs.

Paying for Your Education

"If you think education is expensive, try ignorance."

Derek Bok

How can you afford the cost of an education if money is already tight? You may be able to finance your education with help from the federal government, which offers a variety of grants, low-interest loans, and work-study programs. For specific information about help from the federal government, call 800-433-3243. To find out whether the school you're considering participates in any of the federal government's student assistance programs, contact the school's financial aid office or call the number above.

Your state may also fund and administer its own education assistance programs. Call your state department of education, or talk to the financial aid office at the school you'd like to attend.

Federal Loans

Here is a short overview of the federal loans you may be eligible for:

Perkins loan.   This 5 percent interest loan is available to both undergraduate and graduate students with exceptional financial need. Full-time and part-time students are eligible.

Stafford loan.   This low-interest loan is for students attending school at least half-time. Subsidized loans are awarded on the basis of financial need; unsubsidized loans don't consider financial need. You can have both at the same time.

Supplemental loan for students (SLS).   Both undergraduate and graduate students are eligible for this variable-rate loan.

If you get a federal loan to help you finance your education, you must start repaying it soon after you complete your education, regardless of whether you locate a job in the field you hoped to be working in or have increased your income.

Federal Grants

Unlike a loan, you won't have to repay a grant—it's a gift. Therefore, grants tend to be more difficult to get. Following are some of the federal grants you may want to apply for.

Pell grant.   Undergraduate students who have not earned bachelors or professional degrees and who attend school at least half-time can apply. Eligibility is based on financial need.

Supplemental Educational Opportunity Grant (SEOG).
The SEOG is available to undergraduates who can demonstrate exceptional financial need. Students with Pell grants get priority. Full-time and part-time students are eligible.

Hot Tip _____

The U.S. Department of Education (DOE) publishes an excellent overview of its education assistance programs—*The Student Guide to Federal Financial Aid.* Updated annually, the guide can be obtained by calling 800-433-3243, by writing to the Federal Student Aid Programs, P.O. Box 84, Washington, DC 20044, or at DOE's web site, http://www.ed.gov.

Federal Work-Study Programs

Federal work-study programs help undergraduate and graduate students pay for their education by providing them with on-campus and off-campus jobs.

Hot Tip

No matter what kind of educational loan you apply for, work out a realistic budget beforehand so you borrow as little as possible.

Other Sources of Financial Assistance

Your gender, religion, academic or professional achievements, artistic abilities, or other noted characteristics may make you eligible for a special scholarship or grant. To find out what is available, talk to a financial aid officer at the school you'd like to attend, review a directory of scholarships and grants at your local library, or get a copy of *Higher Education Opportunities for Minorities and Women.* For price and ordering information, call 202-219-5577. If you're a veteran, contact your regional Department of Veterans Affairs (VA) office and your state VA office to learn whether you're eligible for any other assistance.

Government Job Assistance

Depending on your circumstances and needs, you may be able to take advantage of federally sponsored employment assistance and job-training programs. They include the following:

Job Training Partnership Act (JTPA). The JTPA provides job-training and employment assistance to economically disadvantaged and dislocated workers. Its services are planned and delivered locally through partnerships between private and public organizations. The focus of each local service delivery system is the Private Industry Council (PIC). To find out about the services available in your area and whether you might benefit from them, call the PIC in your area. If you don't see a listing for a PIC in your local phone book, call your governor's office.

Economic Dislocation and Worker Adjustment Assistance Act (EDWAA). This act helps victims of massive layoffs and plant closings who are not likely to find new employment in their previous industries or occupations, the long-term unemployed, those whose unemployment benefits have run out, farmers, and even some displaced homemakers. EDWAA's services include, among other things, job testing and counseling; job development;

job retraining, including classroom and on-the-job instruction; entrepreneurial training; remedial education skill training; job search, placement, and relocation assistance; and child care and transportation allowances. Because every state administers its services differently, the best way to learn more about your state's EDWAA policies is to call your governor's office. EDWAA is part of JTPA.

Hot Tip ————————————————————

Veterans should call their nearest U.S. Department of Labor, Veteran's Employment and Training Service office to find out about any job-related assistance for which they may be eligible.

The Clean Air Transition Assistance Program.   Also part of JTPA, this program targets workers who have lost their jobs due to their employers' compliance with the Clean Air Act. To be eligible for assistance, workers must meet the EDWAA eligibility criteria. The program's services mirror those provided by EDWAA.

The Defense Conversion Adjustment Program.   This program assists workers who have lost their jobs due to reduced military expenditures or the closure of a military facility. It, too, is part of JTPA, and the services it provides are the same as EDWAA's.

To learn more about these government job programs or any other federal job programs you may be eligible for, write the Office of Employment and Training Programs, U.S. Department of Labor, 200 Constitution Ave., N.W., Rm. N4469, Washington, DC 20210. To learn about any special programs your state may offer, call your state government's listing for Employment and Training, Job or Employment Services, Employment Security Commission, Human Services, or Job Services.

Moonlighting

"Two men look out through the same bars. One sees the earth, and one sees the stars."

F. Langbridge

The number of people moonlighting, or working at another job to earn extra money, is growing, especially among professionals. It seems that everyone—including teachers, college-educated professionals, lawyers, social workers, and even doctors—needs extra money! Moonlighting may involve working a night or a weekend job, working as a freelancer or an independent contractor, or finding extra work through a temporary agency.

Freelancing.   Working as a freelancer involves selling your skills or services directly to clients. For example, you might become a freelance writer, graphic artist, photographer, business consultant, bookkeeper, or data entry person. Freelancers usually work alone, often out of their homes, market themselves to get work, and handle their own client billings and collections.

Independent contracting.   Independent contractors work on a project or contract basis for companies and nonprofit organizations. They are often hired to handle special projects that businesses don't have the in-house expertise to accomplish or that their employees may not have the time to handle. However, as a way to save money, a growing number of private-sector employers now "outsource" or use independent contractors to handle certain business functions or activities their employees used to do. Outsourcing allows them to cut their payrolls.

Some opportunities to do unskilled contract work are advertised in the employment classifieds section of newspapers under part-time or general work. Skilled and professional contract work may also be advertised in newspapers, as well as in professional publications and via word of mouth.

Temporary work.   Temp work involves working for a company or an organization on a nonpermanent basis. Although this kind of work may be advertised in the employment classifieds section of your local newspaper, you can also find such work through a temporary agency. Some agencies place workers with general office and computer skills, while others specialize in placing workers with specific types of skills, including medical and high-tech professionals. Call the temporary agencies in your area to find out which ones place workers with your skills and education. Also, to maximize your temporary employment opportunities, register with several agencies.

Hot Tip

If you have a good relationship with your former employer, contact that person to find out whether he or she uses independent contractors or freelancers. You may be able to sell back your skills and knowledge to your old company.

Hot Tip

Working for a temporary agency can be a good way to identify companies you'd like to work for on a full-time basis or what sort of work you'd enjoy doing if you're thinking about changing careers. It's on-the-job research. Also, if you work out well at a firm, you may have a foot in the door if a full-time job opens up at the company you temp for.

Starting a Part-Time Business

"It is the business of the very few to be independent; it is the privilege of the strong."

Friedrich Nietzsche

Some people earn extra money with a part-time business. It's possible that your part-time business can end up being so emotionally and financially rewarding that eventually it becomes your main source of income.

Having a good business idea is basic to starting a successful business. In addition, to turn your idea into a money maker, even on a relatively small scale, you'll need a unique combination of drive, self-discipline, energy, organizational skills, and solid entrepreneurial know-how, not to mention luck. Most likely, you'll have to have some seed or start-up capital, too.

Before you even begin thinking about possible businesses you might start, it's critical that you spend some time seriously considering whether self-employment is a realistic option for you. Do you have what it takes to be your own boss, or is it something you want to do because you think it sounds glamorous and exciting or because some of your friends are doing it? Remember, self-employment is not easy, and more small businesses fail than succeed.

Many books and magazines discuss business ownership. Read them to help you determine whether you have the personal characteristics necessary for success as your own boss. (See the "Resources" section of this book for some suggested titles.) Not everyone does, and it's better to discover that you don't *before* you've invested your time, energy, and money in a business, not after.

It's important that you realize that a part-time business probably will not provide you with additional cash right away—it may take a couple of years before you see a profit. Also, what cash it does generate may need to be reinvested in your business at first. Sure, some businesses are overnight successes, but they're rare.

Deciding What Your Business Will Be

If you decide that you've got what it takes to start and run a part-time business and that you can afford to gamble on its success, you must decide what kind of business to start. You may already have a specific business in mind, or you may need to research the possibilities. In addition to reading books and magazines, consider brainstorming with friends and relatives. They can be good sounding boards for ideas and may be able to evaluate your business ideas more objectively than you can.

There may be a solid business idea in your hobbies, the things you enjoy doing, or your work skills and experiences. For example, do you love to entertain and cook for others? If so, you might consider catering or party planning. Are you an accountant? Perhaps that skill could provide the basis for a business. Do you have a computer system at home? If so, you could do data entry work, produce company newsletters, or handle wordprocessing and mailings for other businesses, among other things. Do you have a marketable craft? Some states have programs designed to promote local crafts by helping craftspeople market their products; some even offer low-interest loans to craftspeople. To find out whether your state runs such a program, call your governor's office. Gardening and yard work are other things you could do on a part-time basis.

Think about needs that are not being met by current businesses—you may be able to start a business that helps fill a gap. Also, keep your business idea as simple as possible. The more complicated it will be to get it up and running, the more equipment and supplies you will need and the more expensive it will be to get started. Try to identify business possibilities that make good use of the resources you already have on hand.

Factors to Consider

"The beginning is the most important part of any business."

Plato

Because most home-based businesses are relatively inexpensive to start and run, and because technology has made sophisticated office equipment readily available to the home-based entrepreneur, the rest of this chapter assumes that your small business will be home-based. However, like the business startup information preceding this, much of what follows applies to non-home-based businesses as well.

Once you have a list of business possibilities, it's time to determine their feasibilities. Start by identifying the specific space and location requirements of each idea. Following are some of the factors to consider:

Your home's location.   If a business's success depends on volume sales, it's more apt to thrive if you live in a highly populated area. The exception would be a business that relies on catalogue sales or other direct marketing methods. Also, if a business's success depends on high visibility and your home is on a relatively untraveled road or is difficult to see from the road, the business probably is not a viable option unless you can identify inexpensive ways of calling people's attention to your location.

Your home's size.   If your home is relatively small or you already use most of its space, a business that requires room for storing inventory, supplies, or equipment, for employing staff, or for accommodating customers may not be realistic.

Parking.   Assess your parking needs, and find out whether your local government has regulations regarding business parking.

Zoning.   Check with your local government to find out whether the zoning ordinances in your area allow you to operate a home-based business and, if so, whether any restrictions exist on the kind of business you're thinking about.

Up-front capital.   How much money will you need to get a business under way? Err on the high side because unexpected or overlooked expenses are almost inevitable. If a particular business requires a significant investment in equipment, supplies, or inventory, you should probably eliminate it from your list.

Sources of financing.   Where will your startup capital come from? Depending on your financial situation, you may be able to get a loan from a bank or through a federal or state loan program. To find out what's available, call the Small Business Administration (SBA) (800-U-ASK-SBA), your state office of economic development, or your state commerce department.

Another option is to use your savings, cash in some investments, or borrow money from a relative or close friend. However, don't do any of these things unless you feel certain that your business has a real chance of success. Also, even if you borrow money from a family member or friend, put the terms of your loan in writing and collateralize the loan so if you end up in bankruptcy, the person who loaned you money will have a better chance of being repaid.

Competition.   Check out the competition. What other businesses offer the same products or services as you're considering? Can your business meet an unanswered need? Can you offer something unique or different that will attract customers and increase your chance for success?

Staff.   Will you need employees to help you? If so, how many? Will they be part time or full time? Will they need to work out of your home?

Taxes.   What taxes will you have to pay, and when will they be due?

Permits.   Will you need to purchase any local, county, or state permits? How much will they cost?

Marketing.   Who and where are your customers? How will you let them know about your business? Advertising, direct mail, promotions, publicity, newsletters, special events, and even the Internet are possibilities. You will need to allocate a certain amount of money each month for marketing. Often overlooked or underbudgeted by first-time business owners, marketing is generally not a one-time effort.

Hot Tip _____

Before you begin your venture, prepare a business plan that presents your business concept; describes your target market and your competition; discusses how your business will be distinguished from its competitors and how you will market its product or service to your target market; and projects sales, revenues, and cash flow for your business's first several years of operation. This is essential planning and management information. Also, most banks will want to see it if you apply for a loan.

Insurance and bookkeeping.   What insurance will you need? Talk to your insurance broker. How will you handle your book-keeping needs, pay your creditors, generate monthly cash flow statements (monitoring your cash flow every month will be critical), and create other financial statements you'll need to monitor the health of your business?

Estimated expenses and sales.   Project expenses and sales revenues on a month-by-month basis for at least the first year to help determine a business's financial feasibility.

Read and learn as much as you can before you go into business. Enroll in a basic business management class at a college or university in your area, and call your local chamber of commerce to find out what assistance it may be able to offer you. Contact the local office of the SBA. The SBA publishes many free and low-cost publications related to starting and running a business, and many local SBA offices offer seminars and free consultations on various aspects of self-employment. The SBA also sponsors the Service Corps of Retired Executives (SCORE), retired business owners and managers who volunteer their time to provide guidance and education to small-business owners. If you can't locate an SBA office in your local phone book, call 800-U-ASK-SBA, or write the SBA, Office of Consumer Affairs, 409 3rd St., S.W., Washington, DC 20146.

Hot Tip _____

For an upbeat but practical and realistic book about starting and running a successful small business, read *The Small Business Survival Kit: 134 Troubleshooting Tips for Success,* John Ventura, Dearborn Financial Publishing, Inc., 1994.

Be on the Alert for Scams

"A man who is always ready to believe what he is told will never do well."

Gaius Petronius

In your search to make more money, be wary of opportunities that sound too good to be true. They could be scams. Common scams include ads for "guaranteed" well-paying jobs, for work-at-home opportunities, and for business "opportunities" that claim you'll earn big bucks. Typically, to take advantage or these so-called opportunities, you must call a 900 telephone number. (When you call a 900 number, you are charged a flat fee, a per-minute rate, or a combination. All are expensive.) Sometimes you must pay substantial money up front.

You may learn about these opportunities on the radio, in the employment section of your local newspaper, through a mailing, from a telemarketer, or on TV. Although what you are promised may sound enticing, in reality, what you get for your time and money is of little or no value. There is no such thing as easy money.

If a money-making opportunity sounds and looks legitimate, check it out before you pay money or sign any paperwork. Ask for a written statement from the advertiser describing exactly what is being offered and what your obligations to the company will be and spelling out all of your costs. Check out the advertiser with the Better Business Bureau in your town and in the town where the advertiser is located. Also contact your state attorney general's office or office of consumer affairs and this same office in the state where the company is located. Ask for the names and phone numbers of people already pursuing this same opportunity. If you've been victimized by one of these companies, see Figure 3.7 for suggestions on where to go for help.

Hot Tip _____

The U.S. Postal Inspection Service says it "knows of no work-at-home scheme that produces income as alleged."

Part-Time Sales

When thinking about the kinds of part-time businesses you might run out of your home, you may want to consider part-time sales. The work can be lucrative and the hours extremely flexible. However, before investing in this kind of business, be sure that you like to sell because no product, no matter how good, sells itself. To make money, you have to hustle. Also, don't assume you can make enough money by selling only to your friends and family members.

Numerous part-time sales opportunities exist, many with well-established, reputable national firms. Depending on the product, you may make sales through at-home parties, one-on-one sales calls, mailings, seminars and conferences, formal presentations, or advertising. Many of these companies are multilevel marketing firms, which means you can make money by recruiting new representatives for the company and by making sales.

FIGURE 3.7   If You're Victimized by a Business Opportunity Scheme

First, write the company and ask for your money back. Let the company know that if a refund is not forthcoming, you will inform the proper authorities of the problem. If your letter does not have the desired effect, contact the following:

- Your state attorney general's office or office of consumer affairs and the equivalent office in the state where the company is located
- Your local Better Business Bureau and the one in the town where the company is located
- The postmaster in your area (The U.S. Postal Service investigates fraudulent mail practices.)
- The advertising sales manager of the publication running the ad to which you responded
- The Federal Trade Commission

Some of the older and more established part-time sales companies include those that follow:

Amway.   This company offers a diverse array of household products. In addition, as an Amway representative, you can sell other companies' products, including long-distance services, legal services, and home mortgages. To become an Amway representative, you must be recruited by a distributor in your area. Find one listed in your local phone book, or call 800-879-4732.

Tupperware.   This company helped make home sales parties famous. To get started as a Tupperware dealer, you must purchase a sales kit. Although you will be required to pay your state's sales tax up front, you may pay for the rest of the kit through the sales you make. The Tupperware Company provides training for new dealers and organizes an introductory party during which new dealers learn sales techniques. You can earn a 35 percent commission on sales, but you'll have to pay your own expenses, including party hostess gifts. Call 800-858-7221 for more information.

Discovery Toys.   This company also uses parties as sales tools. Company training for new sales consultants includes a manual, a video, and the advice and supervision of a manager. As a sales consultant, you must hold five parties and purchase a sales kit. An up-front fee of $50 covers the kit, tax, and shipping. Sales commissions pay the cost of the kit. Call 800-426-4777.

Mary Kay Cosmetics.   Sales representatives for this international company sell beauty products through at-home beauty consultations. Representatives are educated about company products and trained in sales techniques through sales aids and periodic meetings. Call 800-MARY-KAY.

Avon.   As every reader probably knows, when Avon calls, the salesperson will try to sell you cosmetics and other beauty products. Avon products are sold face to face and through a catalogue. Your up-front investment to sell Avon products is relatively small, less than $50, and your sales commissions begin at 30 percent. Call 800-336-2130.

Shaklee.   This company sells vitamins and environmentally sound home products. To become a sales representative, you must be sponsored by a current representative. Sales training and seminars are provided by Shaklee. Call 800-359-7318.

Stanley Home Products.   Stanley sales representatives sell a variety of personal and household products, including vitamins, fragrances, and cleaning items. Sales representatives can get started for a relatively small initial investment—as little as $20. As a new representative, you'll get a 45 percent commission on your sales. Call 800-628-9032.

Should you decide that you want to pursue part-time sales, find out all you can about the company you want to sell for. Ask questions, read company literature, and talk to current sales representatives. Also, call your state attorney general's office or office of consumer affairs to find out whether any complaints have been filed or actions taken against the part-time sales company that most interests you.

Government Help

"Can anybody remember when the times were not hard and money scarce?"

Ralph Waldo Emerson

Sometimes, when money is tight, you have no alternative but to apply for government assistance. While accepting this kind of help may be something you never imagined you'd have to do, government assistance is sometimes necessary. And remember, it's your tax dollars that help fund these government programs. Descriptions of some of the broader-based federal assistance programs follow.

At the time this book was written, the welfare system was being overhauled. Therefore, the programs and services discussed in this section may no longer be available as described. If you need government assistance to help you get through financial hard times, call your state social services or welfare department to find out exactly what is available to you.

Unemployment Insurance

Unemployment insurance is a federal and state-sponsored program administered by the individual states. It makes cash payments to workers who lose their jobs. Typically, payments are available for 26 weeks, although some states offer extended benefits—up to 39 additional weeks, in some cases. Each state sets its own benefit amounts and eligibility requirements, but generally, if you left your job voluntarily, you are not eligible for this kind of help. However, if you quit your job because of a problem in the workplace—for example, sexual harassment or unsafe working conditions—you are able to collect benefits if you can prove good cause for quitting. Making your case can take time and may require legal help.

To apply for benefits, contact the office that administers your state's unemployment insurance program. It will be listed in your local phone book under Unemployment Insurance, Unemployment Compensation, Employment Security, or Employment Service. If you begin receiving benefits, you must prove that you're actively looking for work to continue receiving them.

If you're denied benefits, you can appeal, and your appeal will be heard at an informal administrative hearing. Witnesses who can substantiate your reasons for receiving unemployment benefits should attend the hearing with you. Also, bring any documentation that supports your claim.

Aid to Families with Dependent Children (AFDC)

AFDC provides cash payments and other assistance to low-income families with dependent children. Dependent children are defined as those who lack the support of one or both parents due to separation, divorce, desertion, death, or imprisonment.

AFDC is both a federal and a state program. The federal government gives funds to the states and sets broad guidelines for the use of those funds. The states then set their own eligibility criteria, including the amount of monthly household income a family can have and the dollar value of its assets, excluding a home and an auto. Some states also exclude a certain amount of clothing and furniture as countable assets.

Each AFDC recipient is required to participate in his or her state's Job Opportunities and Basic Skills Training (JOBS) program as a condition of eligibility. The program provides job training, work assistance, and education opportunities. Some states place other requirements and restrictions on AFDC recipients.

The AFDC Unemployed Parent Program was created in 1988 to provide funds to families with children when the primary income earner is unemployed, underemployed, or disabled.

To find out more about AFDC programs, contact your state's department of human services or social services.

Food Stamps

The food stamp program helps eligible households supplement the amount of food they can afford to buy each month. It also provides employment and job-training services to food stamp recipients. The U.S. Department of Agriculture sets national standards for the program, and local or state welfare or social service agencies administer it locally.

The federal government limits the amount of monthly income a household can earn and the total value of the assets it can own to be eligible to receive food stamps. Generally, a household's monthly income must be at or below 100 percent of federal poverty guidelines. Presently, a family of four cannot have a gross monthly income of more than $1,642 or a net of $1,050. The total dollar value of the food stamps an eligible household receives is based on the number of persons in the household.

Social Security Programs

Disability benefits.   Disability benefits are available to eligible individuals with physical or mental impairments that are expected to prevent them from doing any *substantial* work for at least one year, as well as to persons with medical conditions that are expected to result in death. These benefits are part of the Social Security program. To qualify, at the time of disability, the individual must have worked for at least five out of the last ten years and been paying into the Social Security system. Family members may also be eligible to receive assistance once the disabled person begins collecting payments. It usually takes five months between the time an application for benefits is filed and the time benefits are approved and initiated.

Survivors benefits.   Survivors benefits under the Social Security program may be payable to members of a family when its wage earner dies. However, the wage earner must have been paying into the Social Security system. Benefits are tied to the wages of the former earner. The more that person earned, the larger the payment, up to a maximum amount.

Supplemental Security Income (SSI).   SSI makes monthly payments to individuals who are age 65 or older as well as to adults and children who are blind or disabled. For an individual to be eligible, the dollar value of his or her income and assets cannot exceed the limit established by the state where that person lives.

For details and eligibility information about any of these Social Security assistance programs, contact your local Social Security office, or call 800-772-1213.

Low-Income Home Energy Assistance Program (HEAP)

HEAP provides low-income households with heating, cooling, and weatherization assistance. Persons receiving AFDC, SSI, or food stamps are eligible to participate, as are others who meet the program's eligibility guidelines. HEAP is funded through federal grants to the states. Payments are made directly to eligible households or to home energy suppliers that comply with the program's provisions.

To get details and eligibility criteria for the HEAP in your state, contact your state's department of human services or social services.

Blues Busters

The American dream is to earn enough money at a job you enjoy to live a comfortable lifestyle. It sounds simple, but it gets harder all of the time. However, the information in this chapter can help you assess your options for making more or for finding a new job if you've lost yours. This chapter also provides an overview of the government programs that can help you. Although most people will do everything possible to avoid having to accept government help, sometimes those programs can serve as critical financial safety nets.

FOUR

Keeping Your Wheels on the Road

"More than any other country, ours is an automotive society."
Lyndon Baines Johnson

After being laid off from his full-time job, Jim S. began a consulting business, and his wife Shelley returned to work as a part-time teacher. They came to see me because one of their two cars had become so unreliable that they could no longer count on it as a regular source of transportation. They wanted to discuss options for getting a new car.

"I don't know what to do," Jim told me. "Because I'm self-employed and have been in business only six months, I doubt that I can get a loan from my bank to buy a car, and Shelley isn't making a lot of money. While we have money in savings that we could use, I'm reluctant to touch it because we may need to use those funds to help us pay some important bills, depending on how my business does. We've never been in this situation before. What do you think we should do?"

I had no simple answer to that question. I talked to Jim and Shelley about their options and how to determine the best one for them. We discussed the feasibility of spending money on repairing their car even though it was quite old and they were both tired of it. We also talked about whether Shelley could carpool with someone from school or take public transportation. Although I couldn't make the decision for them, Jim and Shelley left with a better idea of their transportation options and how to evaluate them.

After buying a home, the purchase of a car is the next most significant financial transaction most Americans make. For many, it is their single most important purchase. Yet despite its importance, most consumers approach car buying with little or none of the information they need to objectively evaluate their options so they can make intelligent buying decisions. Too frequently, even when money is tight, their decisions are based on advertising, impulse, and emotion.

It's likely that during the time you live on a tight budget, with little money to spare, you will have to decide whether to

- get a vehicle repaired;
- keep your current car or get a new one;
- buy a used or a new car; or
- lease a new car.

Although decisions about transportation are almost never easy when you have little money to go around, having the right information and knowing how to systematically analyze your options will certainly help.

Should You Keep Your Old Car or Get a New One?

To determine whether you should get another car or keep your current one, compare the costs of owning and maintaining your current car for the number of years you would like to keep it with the ownership and maintenance costs of the car you would buy in its place. To do this, list all the costs and considerations discussed in this section on a sheet of paper. Plug in general dollar amounts for your current car, and compare them to the general costs of the car you want to replace it with.

Ownership Costs

In general, the cost of owning a car decreases as the age of your car increases. This is due to several factors, including depreciation, insurance, finance charges, taxes, and registration. However, your operating costs may increase.

Depreciation.   Cars and certain other assets depreciate, or lose value, as they age due to simple wear and tear. Cars usually depreciate the most during the early years of ownership. The more your car depreciates, the lower its resale or trade-in value will be. Unless you anticipate that your car will need some especially costly repairs in the near future, holding on to it may be a good idea because, depending on its age and make, you probably will not make much money if you sell it.

Insurance.   The older your car, the lower your collision and comprehensive insurance costs will be because the car will be worth less due to depreciation. In fact, once your car is five to six years old, you may want to consider canceling your collision insurance and paying for liability coverage only.

Finance charges.   Auto loans are structured in such a way that the amount of equity you have in your car grows slowly. In the early stages, your car payments go primarily toward the interest on your loan, not the principal; therefore, you probably owe more on your car than it's worth. Consequently, unless your car payments are too high and you simply need to get a car that costs you less each month, it probably wouldn't make a lot of sense to get rid of it if your car is still quite new.

However, at some point, the amount of equity you have in your car begins to exceed the amount of your down payment. Then a new car becomes a more viable option. To determine when your equity exceeds your down payment and exactly how much equity you have in your car, talk to your banker or to the company financing your current vehicle.

If you own your current car outright and plan to finance the purchase of a new one, you'll find that the interest charges on a new loan usually add substantially to the costs of owning a new car. This is yet another reason to hold on to what you've got if at all possible.

To determine your total interest charges, calculate the total dollar value of the car payments you would make over the life of the loan you are considering, and subtract the car's purchase price from that amount.

Taxes and registration.   In some states, the cost of registering your car decreases as the age of your car increases. Also, depending on your state, if your car is taxed as personal property, the tax rate may decline as your car ages and its market value decreases. To learn your state's registration and taxation policies, call your state's department of motor vehicles or your insurance broker.

Operating costs.   In general, the costs of operating your car—repairs, maintenance, and gasoline—will increase as your vehicle ages.

Repairs.   Ask your auto mechanic for an itemized list of the things you'll probably have to fix or replace given the age, make, and model of your car, together with a cost estimate for each, to keep it in running order. Also, ask your mechanic to assess the condition of your car's tires and estimate how soon you will have to replace them given your driving patterns.

Hot Tip ⎯⎯⎯⎯⎯⎯⎯⎯⎯⎯⎯⎯⎯⎯⎯⎯⎯

Review the repair frequency information for your car in the most recent edition of *The Complete Car Cost Guide,* published by IntelliChoice.

You can slow the rate at which your car's operating costs increase by giving your vehicle regular care and maintenance. If you have the owner's manual, refer to the list of maintenance activities it recommends. If you don't have a manual, talk to your mechanic or a dealer in your area that sells your make of car. Any problem your car has should be diagnosed and repaired as soon as possible; delay can result in more costly repairs.

Getting your car repaired can be an expensive and frustrating experience unless you know how to protect yourself from over-priced, incompetent repair shops. Here are some tips for mini-mizing car repair hassles:

- Check your car's warranty or service contract. Does it place any restrictions on where and how your car is repaired?
- In the case of a major repair, shop around. Ask several re-pair shops for written estimates. Get in writing each shop's hourly rate and any exceptions to that rate.
- Tell the shops you visit what your car's symptoms are, not what needs to be fixed. Let each shop diagnose the problem.
- Check a shop's complaint record before working with it. Do this by calling your area's Better Business Bureau.

Hot Tip

All states have *lemon laws* for new cars with recurring prob-lems. Check with your state's attorney general's office or office of consumer affairs about the laws in your state.

- Ask if new or rebuilt parts will be used. Many high-quality rebuilt parts are available today that can save you consid-erable money.
- Find out whether a shop offers a warranty. If so, does it cover both parts and labor? Is there a price difference be-tween new and rebuilt parts? Get any warranties in writing.
- Before you leave your car at a shop, make sure that the work order reflects what needs to be done.
- Ask that the shop contact you before it makes any repairs not listed on the work order. If it fails to do so, you do not have to pay for the unauthorized work, and you have the right to get your bill adjusted.
- Keep copies of all work orders and receipts.

Maintenance.   Maintenance activities for your car include things like brake jobs, engine tune-ups, and oil changes. Using the same time period as you use for estimating the total cost of future repairs to your car, calculate your probable maintenance costs. Do this by reviewing the maintenance schedule recom-mended by the manufacturer, getting cost estimates from your auto mechanic, and taking your driving conditions into account.

Gasoline.   You can estimate the amount of money you will spend on fuel by multiplying the number of miles your car currently gets per gallon by the number of miles per year you expect to drive your car over the years you want to keep it.

If Getting Another Car Is the Best Option

"If you don't know where you are going, you will probably end up someplace else."

Laurence Peter

If replacing your current car turns out to be your best option, you'll have a whole new set of considerations to address. The most important will be your budget, your transportation needs, and financing.

Using your spending plan as a guide, determine how much you can afford to spend on another car. Can you afford to make regular monthly payments on a new car, or will you need to find a used car that you can buy outright? Do you have money in savings earmarked for a down payment on a car? Can you revise your spending plan to accommodate the purchase of a car? What is your current car's approximate trade-in or resale value?

Hot Tip

If you live in a city with good public transportation, or if you can commute to work by bike or on foot, you may be able to delay buying a new car. If you will need a car occasionally, taking taxis—or even renting a car—may be cheaper than ownership; or maybe a friend or relative would lend you a car. While this approach to transportation may not be good for the long haul, it may be worth considering for a while.

Consider also how you will use the car you buy. For example, how many people will it need to carry? Will you chauffeur a lot of kids? Will you take clients in it? Do you need something that can carry equipment, supplies, or portable baby furniture? Do you travel long distances in your work? Are you in a car pool?

Once you've defined your transportation needs and budget, it's time to evaluate the pros and cons of your options for getting a car. They include buying a new car, buying a used car, and leasing a car.

Figure 4.1 presents the advantages and disadvantages of each option.

Doing Your Research

Read car buying guides and magazines to determine the makes and models that best fit your transportation needs and budget. Eliminate those that get poor gas mileage or that have poor repair and maintenance records.

Once you've narrowed down your options, get some current price information. If you're shopping for a new car, obtain the manufacturer's suggested retail price and the dealer's invoice price. If you're looking for a used car, determine its market value. This information will help you recognize a good car deal when you see one and will make you a better negotiator when you're ready to buy a car. A good source of general information on new car costs is *Edmund's New Car Prices*, available in most public libraries. While actual prices vary and need to be determined when you visit dealers, this publication is a good place to start.

Hot Tip —————————————————

If you belong to a credit union, find out whether it uses AutoFacts. This free service offers information on car prices, gas usage, repair records, and affordability.

Carputer International is another excellent source of information. This company sells car pricing information on specific cars, including the manufacturer's suggested retail price, the dealer or invoice price, factory options and their costs, and any rebate information available. For a small fee, Carputer International will send you a detailed report on a specific make and model of car. To get pricing information and specific details on what the company offers, call 800-992-7404.

For used-car pricing information, the best source is the *Official Used Car Guide*, known as the *Blue Book*, published by the National Automobile Dealers Association and available at most local libraries and car dealerships. The *Blue Book* provides average trade-in, loan, and retail prices for specific used cars. However, *Blue*

FIGURE 4.1   Transportation Pros and Cons

New Car

Pros

- Repairs and servicing covered by warranty in early years
- Generally fewer problems than with a used car
- With each loan payment, equity builds in an asset that has cash value
- Lower operating costs than with a used car

Cons

- Ownership costs higher than with a used car
- Higher initial costs than with a used or leased car
- Rapid depreciation in early years
- Generally larger monthly payments than with a used or leased car

Used Car

Pros

- Lower ownership costs than with a new car
- Lower monthly costs than with a new or leased car
- Lower initial cost than with a new car, if financing

Cons

- Higher operating costs than with a new car
- Usually a limited warranty or no warranty at all
- Greater chance of mechanical problems than with a new car

Leased Car

Pros

- Generally lower initial cost and monthly payments than with a new car
- Look and reliability of a new car
- Ease of paperwork, registration, and inspection

Cons

- At end of lease period, no car to trade in or sell
- No equity built

Book prices are only approximations because any number of factors, including the region of the country you live in, the time of year, a particular car's condition, and general economic trends, can influence a used car's actual price. A good way to assess the going price for a used car is to review your area's classifieds for asking prices on cars identical or comparable to what you're considering. Keep in mind, however, that if you buy a used car from a dealer, the price you can expect to pay generally will be somewhat higher than what you'll find in the classifieds.

If you will trade in or sell a car, first determine its value because that will affect how much money you'll have to come up with to buy a new car. The resources just discussed will help you price your car. Generally, however, you'll get more money for a car by selling it yourself than by trading it in.

Assessing Your Financing Options

As part of your research, call some potential financing sources to learn what terms they can offer you. Sources of car loans include banks, savings and loans, credit unions, and automobile finance companies such as GMAC and Ford Motor Credit. Find out which dealers offer the best financing packages on the type of car you want to buy. That way, you'll know which dealers to visit in person.

A potential creditor will look at the following factors when deciding whether to give you a car loan:

- Can you come up with a down payment—in cash, as a trade-in, or a combination of these?
- Do you have a steady job?
- Do you meet your current obligations?
- If you filed a Chapter 7 bankruptcy, did you reaffirm your debts? If you filed a Chapter 13, do you meet the terms of your reorganization plan?
- What was your credit history before your bankruptcy or before your money troubles? And why did you get into financial trouble? Was it due to overspending or job loss, for example?

Hot Tip ————————————————————

If you are currently in a Chapter 13 bankruptcy, you must have approval from the courts before you can take on any new debt, including a car loan.

How to Shop for a Car

Once you have a general idea of what kind of car you want, the financing options available to you and their likely costs, and how much you can afford, it's time to visit some auto dealers. Tell each dealer exactly what you're looking for, and listen to what he or she has to offer. Bring along a notebook and take notes.

Test drive the cars that seem most interesting. Drive them on a variety of roads (highways, hills, smooth and bumpy surfaces) and in a variety of driving conditions (stop-and-go traffic, at highway speed). Note how well they brake, accelerate, and steer. Listen to their radios and tape and CD players, and see how well their heating and cooling systems work. With used cars, check the wear on tires and the condition of both the interior and exterior. Listen for any unusual noises or vibrations.

Ask for the invoice price of the new cars that most interest you. This is the price a dealer pays for a car before any manufacturer rebates, allowances, or discounts. It's an important piece of information. The difference between the manufacturer's suggested retail price for a car and its invoice price represents the dealer's profit margin, and therefore, it's the number to focus on when you negotiate a new car purchase price.

Hot Tip ————————————————————

The invoice price always includes freight charges. If you pay invoice price for a car, ask that the freight charges be deducted.

Also get information from the car dealers you visit about any buyer incentives they offer. These might include cash rebates or discounts, special financing, and option package discounts. Write all this information in your notebook.

When looking at new cars, note that each vehicle has a *Monroney sticker* in its window. Required by federal law, the sticker provides the following information:

- Car's base price, which is the cost of the car without options, including standard equipment, factory warranty, and freight (also known as destination or delivery charges)
- Manufacturer's installed options with the manufacturer's suggested retail prices
- Manufacturer's transportation charge

Information about a car's average fuel economy may be found either on the Monroney sticker or on a separate EPA fuel economy label.

Some dealers also put dealer stickers on their new cars. These are supplemental stickers that state dealer or Monroney sticker prices plus the suggested prices of dealer-installed options—additional dealer profit, dealer preparation, and undercoating, for example.

New Car Warranties

Several types of warranties are available for new cars, ranging from warranties covering all mechanical or other defects for 12 months or 12,000 miles, whichever comes first, to those that provide the same coverage, but for up to four years or 50,000 miles. Some dealers also offer extended warranties for major drivetrain components.

Service contracts and special warranties covering repairs for longer periods of time than basic warranties, or covering repairs not usually included in extended drivetrain warranties, are often available from manufacturers and independent warranty companies.

When evaluating a warranty or a service contract, consider the following questions:

- How long does it last, and when does it start and end?
- What is covered—problems and parts?
- Will it pay for all repair costs, or just for parts or labor?
- Will it pay for parts shipping?
- Will it pay for a loaner car?
- What are my obligations?

- Who will make the repairs?
- How reliable is the company offering the warranty or service contract?
- What sort of cancellation or refund policy does it have?

Hot Tip _____

Some states offer additional warranty rights for consumers. Check with your state attorney general's office or office of consumer affairs.

_____

Regardless of how much pressure you may feel from a car salesperson or how good a deal you are told that you are getting, do not make a purchase decision in a showroom or on a car lot. Instead, after you've finished visiting car dealers, go home, put pencil to paper, and analyze your options. Prioritize the cars you are most drawn to in terms of which best suit your needs and fit your budget. Determine how much above the invoice price, if anything, you would pay for a specific car and what your initial offer would be. Compare the prices and financing packages offered by dealers. If you've not yet done so, determine the trade-in value of your old car if you will make it part of the sale.

Once you've finished your analysis and identified your best options, you are ready to negotiate a purchase price. When you return to a dealer to talk money, start low and negotiate up, but don't go beyond the maximum price you set for a particular car when you did your analysis.

When the dealer counters, it's perfectly all right to say that you need to go home and do some more figuring. If you don't feel comfortable or confident doing the negotiating, ask a trusted friend or relative to do it for you.

Buying a Used Car

Two sources for used cars exist—dealers and private sellers. If you buy from a private seller, you probably will get a better price than if you bought the same car from a dealer. However, when you buy from a dealer, you gain the protection of the Federal Trade Commission's Used Car Rule, which requires that dealers post *Buyers Guide stickers* on their used cars. These stickers provide the following information:

- Whether a car comes with a warranty
- Provisions of any warranty
- General information about the problems that any used car may have
- Suggestion that a buyer have the car inspected by an independent mechanic before purchase
- Warning to get in writing all dealer promises about the car you wish to purchase

If you negotiate any changes in the warranty coverage, make sure those changes are written into your *Buyers Guide.* You will receive the original *Buyers Guide,* or an identical copy, when you buy a used car. It becomes part of your sales contract with the dealer.

Buyers Guide Warranties

A used car can come with one of four types of warranty coverages:

1. No warranty or "as is."   If you buy a used car without a warranty, any problems the car has are yours. The dealer is neither obligated to fix the problems nor pay for the repairs. Some states prohibit "as is" sales. Check with your state attorney general's office or office of consumer affairs about the law in your state.

2. Implied warranties.   Nearly all used cars come with implied, or unwritten, warranties. These warranties are implied by law and are not warranties that dealers themselves offer. Two basic types of implied warranties exist. The most common is the *warranty of merchantability.* This means that the car will do what it is supposed to do—run. The other type of implied warranty is the *warranty of fitness.* This warranty promises that the vehicle is suitable for a particular purpose—traveling through rugged terrain, for example.

3. Dealer warranties.   A dealer may offer a written warranty on a used vehicle. When it does, the dealer must fill in the warranty portion of the *Buyers Guide.* The terms and coverage of a used car warranty are often negotiable.

A dealer's warranty may be either full or limited on all or some of a car's components and systems. Full warranties are rare for used cars. Under a limited warranty, the buyer must pick up some of the costs of repair, and it is likely that some of the car's components are not covered.

The *Buyers Guide* must provide the following information on a full or a limited warranty:

- Percentage of the repair costs the dealer will absorb
- Specific parts and systems covered by the warranty
- Duration of the warranty for each covered system
- Applicable deductibles

The federal Magnuson-Moss Act gives you the right to review a copy of a dealer's warranty before purchasing a vehicle. The warranty provides more detailed information than the *Buyers Guide*. Examine it carefully.

When reviewing the warranty on a used car, pay special attention to whether the dealer or a third party actually fulfills the terms. If it's a third party, check to see whether the company is reputable and insured. Find out the name of the insurer, and call the Better Business Bureau to make sure that it has a good record.

Unexpired manufacturer's warranties.   Used cars sold by dealers and by individuals may come with unexpired manufacturer's warranties or unexpired extended warranties, which means the cars are still covered by those warranties. A dealer may include such a warranty in the systems covered and duration section of the *Buyers Guide*.

If the used car you're considering has one of these warranties, find out what it covers, if it's transferable to a new owner, and, if it is, whether you must pay a fee to get it transferred to your name.

Independent Inspection

Just because a used car looks attractive and comes with a warranty, don't assume that it runs well. Instead, take the car for a test drive, just as you would a new car, and get it inspected by an independent mechanic. Make your offer to buy a car contingent on its passing this inspection or on the sales price being reduced sufficiently to cover the cost of all necessary repairs. Although you'll have to pay for an inspection, it will be money well spent.

Some dealers will allow you to take a used car off the lot to get it inspected, while others will ask that the mechanic come to the lot. If a dealer discourages you from getting the opinion of an independent mechanic or tries to get you to use one that he or she recommends, take it as an indication that the car has mechanical problems, and look for another car at another dealership.

Hot Tip

When you buy a used car, you should receive a written statement of the number of miles the car has been driven. If it's not provided, ask for one. A seller who tampers with a car's odometer or lies about the number of miles a car has been driven is breaking federal law and can be prosecuted.

Buying a Used Car from a Private Seller

If you decide to buy a car from a private seller, you can do a number of things to ensure that you get a good car:

- Ask to see the car's repair and maintenance records. Check to see whether the car has been properly maintained, and review the repair records to identify any problems it may have.
- Ask the owner whether the car has ever been in an accident, and look carefully for signs of an accident, such as mismatched paint and crinkled metal.
- Take the car on a test drive just as you would a new car.
- Take the car to an independent mechanic to have it thoroughly checked out.
- Check the condition of the car's tires.
- Ask to see the car's title. Never buy a car before you see one and know it's legitimate.

Hot Tip

Some states require that both dealers and individual sellers of used cars guarantee that the cars they sell will pass state inspection. Call your state attorney general's office or office of consumer affairs to learn what your state requires of used car dealers and private sellers.

Financing a Car

"This is the only country that went to the poor house in an automobile."

Will Rogers

An auto loan is an installment loan with your car pledged as collateral. As with other such loans, you have to make a series of regular monthly payments in a fixed amount to pay off the loan's principal and interest.

Most car loans are made for a period of two to four years. Some banks now make five-year loans, although they are rarely given for used cars. While a longer loan has the advantage of decreasing the size of your monthly payments, you pay significantly more in interest and therefore, increase the overall cost of the car.

Two factors affect the total amount of money you need to borrow to purchase a car: the value of the car you will trade in, assuming you have one to trade, and the amount of money you have to put down.

Just as you would if you were financing any other purchase, shop around for the financing package with the most advantageous terms. (See Chapter 8 for things to consider when you shop for an installment loan.) In most cases, your best source of financing will be a bank, a savings and loan, or your credit union; however, a dealer may be more willing than other creditors to work with you if you have money troubles.

Dealer Financing

Dealer financing usually comes at a relatively high rate of interest because typically a bank, not the dealer, actually finances the loan. In other words, the dealer borrows money from a bank at one rate of interest and then loans that money to a car buyer at a higher rate of interest. The difference between the dealer's cost of credit and the consumer's cost of credit is profit for the dealer.

A dealer may offer a competitive financing package, but be unwilling to negotiate on price or want a larger than usual down payment. To determine whether a dealer's financing package is a good deal, be sure you understand all its terms and conditions and compare it to your other alternatives. To help you identify your best option, here are some of the questions you should answer:

- Will you have to pay a higher price for a particular car to take advantage of a dealer's financing package?
- Would the car's price be lower if you paid cash or got your financing elsewhere?
- Does the financing package require a larger than usual down payment?
- Are you required to pay the loan in a shorter time than usual—for example, within two to three years?
- To qualify for the financing, do you have to buy something you wouldn't want otherwise? (This could include rust proofing, an extended warranty, or a service contract.)
- Is the financing available for a limited time only?
- Does it apply only to certain cars?
- If a manufacturer's rebate is offered, are you required to give it to the dealer to get the financing?

If the dealer offers special promotions such as high trade-in allowances or free or low-cost options, make sure they're of real value. Check the following:

- Does the high trade-in allowance apply to all cars regardless of their condition?
- Does the high trade-in allowance end up making the car more expensive than it would be without the trade-in?
- Are you getting a better price from the dealer who offers special promotions than you would from one not offering such enticements?
- Do the special promotions apply to cars that have to be ordered or only to those on a dealer's lot?

Most creditors will not make a loan to anyone who can't come up with a cash down payment, a trade-in, or a combination of these. However, you may be able to find a dealer willing to work with you. Typically, such dealers either have a lot of money to lend or really want to move their inventories.

Dealers who do their own financing will sometimes carry a separate note for a down payment. However, these loans usually come with high rates of interest and significant restrictions. Also, some dealers may be willing to cosign your bank loan to help you qualify for the loan.

Service Contracts

When buying either a new or a used car from a dealer, you will probably be offered the opportunity to buy a service contract, or an extended warranty. This offer may be made at the time of purchase or at some time after you've bought your car, and the offer may come from the dealer, the car manufacturer, or an independent company. Whether a service contract is worth the money depends on the answer to a number of key questions:

- Do the service contract and the standard warranty overlap or cover the same things?
- What repairs are covered by the service contract, and what are the conditions of the coverage?
- Who will authorize payment of claims if a repair covered by the service contract has to be made? If a dealer or an administrator will, make sure the company has a solid reputation, and find out how long it has been in business. To do this, call your local Better Business Bureau, your state attorney general's office or office of consumer affairs, or your area's automobile dealers association.
- Is the service contract underwritten by an insurance company? If it is, call your state's insurance commission. This office can tell you whether the insurance company is in good financial shape and whether any complaints have been filed against it.
- Who will make the service contract repairs, and how will payment be made? Be sure that the company making the repairs is convenient to your home or place of employment. Find out whether you will have to pay for the repairs yourself and then get reimbursed for them. If this is the case, be sure that you clearly understand the reimbursement process and how long it generally takes to get reimbursed. Also, find out whether the service contract is good only within a limited geographic area and whether repair and towing services must be authorized before they are used and the process for such authorization.
- What are your responsibilities under the service contract, and what are the conditions of those responsibilities? Will failure to meet these terms and conditions invalidate the contact?

- How much does the service contract cost, and how long does it last? The up-front cost for a service contract ranges from $200 or $300 to $1,000. In many cases, a deductible or fee must be paid every time the car is brought in for work covered by the service contract. Also, ask whether you will be charged a per-repair or per-visit service fee.

If the duration of the service contract is longer than you plan on keeping the car, check whether a shorter contract is available. Also, find out whether you can transfer the contract upon sale of the car and whether any transfer fees apply.

Leasing a Car

"No man-made device since the shield and lance of the knights quite fulfills a man's ego like an automobile."
William Roberts

Leasing a car has become an attractive option for an increasing number of consumers. To determine whether leasing makes sense for you, compare the initial, ongoing, and final costs of leasing to the costs of buying and maintaining the same or an equivalent car. Use the checklist in Figure 4.2 to make this comparison.

Hot Tip _____

If you don't feel comfortable making the comparison yourself, ask your banker, finance company, or a dealer to help you compare the costs of buying and leasing after you have gathered all cost information on each option.

Two basic types of auto leases exist—closed-end and open-end. The closed-end lease is the more user-friendly.

Closed-End Lease

A closed-end lease obligates you to pay a fixed amount of money each month for the period of time specified in your lease contract. At the end of the lease, you return the car and have no further responsibility to the lessor unless you put more than the usual amount of wear and tear on the car or drove it more than the number of miles specified in your lease. In other words, the lessor assumes the risk for the value of the car at the end of your lease.

FIGURE 4.2   Checklist for Comparing Leasing and Purchasing
Costs

After you have selected a new vehicle, you might wish to use this checklist
to help you compare the costs of leasing against the costs of purchasing through
a conventional loan. In making such rough comparisons, you will need to consider three categories of costs: initial; continuing; and final. However, when deciding whether to lease or purchase, you may not want to base your decision
solely on total costs, but also may wish to consider your ability to make the periodic payments and when (or if) any large cash outlays are required.

Initial Costs (At Signing of the Lease)

Leasing		*Purchasing*	
Security deposit	$_____	Down payment	$_____
Capitalized cost reduction, if applicable	_____		
First periodic payment	_____		
Last periodic payment, if applicable	_____		
Total amount of fees (license, registration, and taxes)	_____	Total amount of fees, (license, registration, and taxes)	_____
Trade-in allowance, if applicable	_____	Trade-in allowance, if applicable	_____
Total charges	$_____	Total charges	$_____

Continuing Costs (During the Lease Term)

Leasing		*Purchasing*	
Periodic payment (for example, monthly or weekly)	$_____	Periodic payment (for example, monthly or weekly)	$_____
Insurance (for example, monthly or weekly)	_____	Insurance (for example, monthly or weekly)	_____
Estimated monthly or weekly maintenance or repair costs considering warranty coverage	_____	Estimnated monthly or weekly maintenance or repair costs considering warranty coverage	_____
Total charges	$_____	Total charges	$_____

FIGURE 4.2   Checklist for Comparing Leasing and Purchasing Costs
(Continued)

Final Costs (At Lease End or Upon Early Termination)

*Leasing**		*Purchasing*	
Maximum end-of-lease payment based on estimated residual value**	$_____	Balloon payment, if applicable	$_____
Excessive mileage charge	_____		
Excessive wear charge	_____		
Disposition charge	_____		
Total charges	$_____	Total charges	$_____
Under Early Termination			
Early termination charges	$_____	Early payoff charges	$_____
Total charges	$_____	Total charges	$_____
Other Considerations			
Default charges	$_____	Default charges	$_____
Late charges	$_____	Late charges	$_____

*If you have a purchase option, you may wish to consider the amount of the purchase option price in your comparison.
**For open-end lease only.

Source: Federal Trade Commission, "A Consumer Guide to Vehicle Leasing," 1994.

Open-End Lease

An open-end lease tends to be somewhat cheaper than a closed-end lease on a month-to-month basis. However, when you sign this kind of lease, you gamble that at the end of the lease period, the car will be worth at least as much as the amount specified in the lease agreement. If, due to factors like wear and tear or excess mileage, the car is worth less, you must make an end-of-lease payment to the lessor.

An open-end lease specifies a car's *estimated residual value*, or what it will be worth once you return it to the lessor. At the end of your lease, the lessor will either sell the car or have it appraised and will compare the sales price or the appraisal to the car's estimated residual value. If either the sales price or the appraisal is less than the estimated residual value, you may have to pay all or a percentage of that difference. If either is higher, you may be able to pocket the difference, depending on the terms of your lease. Although it's unlikely that a lessor would sell a car for less than its estimated residual value, you may want to protect yourself by negotiating a lease agreement that gives you the right to approve the final sales price.

The federal Consumer Leasing Act (CLA) gives you the right to hire an independent appraiser to provide a second appraisal if you disagree with the one the lessor gets. However, you must pay the second appraisal, and the appraiser must be acceptable to the lessor. Furthermore, both you and the lessor will be bound by the independent appraisal.

The CLA says that in most instances, the lessor cannot collect any more than three times the average monthly lease payment if the leased car sells or appraises for less than its estimated residual value at the end of the lease. Exceptions exist, however:

- If you agree to pay more than what was specified in the lease agreement
- If the car suffered unreasonable wear and tear while you had it, or if you drove the car more than the number of miles specified in the contract
- If the lessor takes you to court to collect a larger end-of-lease payment and wins

Likely Up-Front Costs

The CLA requires that the lessor indicate in writing all of the up-front costs you must pay before you sign a lease agreement. Usually negotiable, these costs include the following:

Security deposit.   The security deposit protects the lessor should you fail to make your payments, damage the car, or exceed the maximum number of miles stated in your lease contract. If you sign an open-end lease, your deposit could be applied toward your end-of-lease payment.

First and last lease payments.   These payments are usually required at the start of a lease. Depending on the health of your credit record and the policies of the lessor, you may be required to pay more than two months' rent up front.

Capitalized cost reduction.   This is the equivalent of a down payment on a new car. The exact amount you pay depends on the lessor's policies and how good a negotiator you are. It also depends somewhat on your credit record. If your record is not strong, you may have to make a larger than average payment. While doing so lowers the amount of your monthly payments, it may make leasing a less attractive option because you may find that your capitalized cost reduction is close to or more than the amount you would pay as a down payment on a new car.

Hot Tip

To reduce the size of your capitalized cost reduction, consider trading in a car you own.

Sales tax, title, and license.   These are all negotiable items, so the lessor may be willing to pay a portion of them. Some states allow you to spread out these costs over the period of the lease so that they are added to your monthly lease payments. If your state does not explicitly allow this, you may still be able to negotiate something similar for yourself.

Insurance.   Some lessors require that you purchase insurance; others provide it. In either case, the CLA says that the lessor must tell you the type and amount of insurance required.

Ongoing costs of leasing.   If you lease a car, not only might you have to assume responsibility for regular monthly lease payments, but you might have to incur additional regular expenses for such things as repairs and maintenance on the car. These additional costs are usually negotiable.

Monthly payments.   The CLA requires the lessor to disclose certain information about a lease's monthly payments before you sign the lease. These include the

- total number of payments;
- amount of each payment;
- total amount of all payments; and
- payment due date or schedule.

Repairs and Maintenance

Your lease agreement should state clearly exactly who is responsible for repairs and maintenance and should spell out the standards for these services. If it doesn't, before you sign the lease, get the lessor to add this information, including exactly when and where repairs and maintenance activities must take place. Having this clearly defined should help minimize the potential for end-of-lease disputes regarding what constitutes excessive wear and tear on the car.

Hot Tip _____

Terms like *reasonable wear and tear* or *reasonable maintenance* are vague and therefore do not provide you with adequate protection. Get these terms defined in your lease agreement.

End-of-Lease Costs

Final charges are generally negotiable. Because they can significantly affect just how good a deal a lease is, pay careful attention to them. In addition to an end-of-lease payment on an open-end lease, final costs may include the following:

Excessive wear charge.   In most cases, you will be responsible for the cost of repair if, at the end of the lease, your car has suffered excessive wear and tear. The amount of the charge or the method used to calculate that charge must be spelled out in your lease.

Excess mileage charge.   Most closed-end leases establish a maximum mileage allowance for the term of a lease. If you exceed that maximum, you must pay an additional fee when you return the car. If you do a lot of driving, be sure that you negotiate a sufficiently high maximum mileage allowance.

Default penalties.   Default penalties come into play if you're unable to meet the terms of your lease—for example, if you can't make your monthly payments on schedule or you stop making payments entirely. Your lease should clearly state what happens in this event. Default penalties might include losing a security deposit, a demand for payment in full of all your lease obligations, and payment of any legal fees and costs the lessor incurs to get the vehicle back.

Disposition charges. These include cleaning costs, tune-ups, and maintenance on a car once it's returned to the lessor and is prepared for sale. Such costs may be charged to you.

Option Rights

A lease typically gives you a series of options that you can exercise during or at the end of your lease. These may include the right to purchase the car you've leased, the right to renew or extend your lease, and early termination.

Purchase option. If your lease includes a purchase option, the CLA requires that the lessor tell you the estimated residual value of the car and the formula used to calculate the car's purchase price before you sign the lease agreement. Purchase options are most closely associated with open-end leases.

If you would like a purchase option that is not part of the lease you will sign, ask that it be included. Otherwise, negotiating for a purchase option at the end of your lease will be entirely separate from the lease itself, and purchase terms may not be as advantageous as if they had been negotiated at the outset.

Renewal option. Your lease should include an option to extend or renew. If a lessor knows at the onset that you may want to lease on a month-to-month basis after your lease term is up, you probably will be able to negotiate lower monthly payments.

Other Lease Considerations

Warranties. The lessor is also required by the CLA to disclose in writing information about the warranty for a leased car. The lessor must state whether the standard manufacturer's warranty is in effect and whether the lessor provides additional warranties. You will be required to follow a certain maintenance schedule to keep the warranty in effect.

Many lessors also offer extended service plans or contracts to cover instances where the warranty ends before the lease term is up.

Extended service plans.   If a lessor offers an extended service plan for repairs and maintenance at an additional cost to you, carefully compare the car's standard warranty with the extended plan. Compare what each covers to the repairs and maintenance activities you are responsible for. It is possible that you will be able to fulfill your obligation for repairs and maintenance through an extended service plan.

Hot Tip

If you renew your lease for more than four months or extend it for more than six months, the CLA says that the lessor is required once again to give you all the disclosures you received at the start of the lease.

Early termination.   The CLA says that the lessor must tell you before you sign a lease when you can terminate and what the early termination cost will be. In most cases, you will not be able to end a lease before 12 months.

Hot Tip

For more information about leasing a car, including specific questions to ask a lessor before you sign an agreement and worksheets for comparing the costs of buying and leasing, order *A Consumer Guide to Vehicle Leasing* from the Federal Trade Commission. This free brochure is available by writing the FTC, 6th and Pennsylvania Aves., N.W., Washington, DC 20580.

If You Decide to Lease a Car

Once you have decided to lease, list the cars you are most interested in, and contact local auto leasing companies for leasing information. Many new car dealers also lease cars, and you may want to call them as well. Ask about the types and terms of leases each company offers. Based on what you learn over the phone, select the companies you think are worth visiting.

When you negotiate a car lease, keep in mind the costs that are generally negotiable so that you can get the best deal possible. If you don't feel comfortable doing the negotiating, ask a friend or relative to help you.

Contact the National Vehicle Leasing Association at 800 Airport Blvd., Suite 506, Burlingame, CA 94010, 800-225-6852, as well as your local Better Business Bureau before you do business with a specific auto leasing company to make sure no complaints have been lodged against it.

Blues Busters

For most of us, having proper transportation is essential. However, if you live from paycheck to paycheck or if your credit is poor, affording good, reliable transportation can be a problem. Therefore, whether you need to get a car repaired, buy a second car, or replace your existing car, it's essential that you do up-front research so that you get the best deal you can afford and don't get taken. That means you need to know the questions to ask and what to look for when you get your car repaired. And if you buy a new or used car, it means that you learn everything you can about the models you're considering and that you compare your options so you can make a wise decision.

FIVE

Knowing Your Rights If Things Go Wrong

*"*Government is too big and too important to be left to the politicians.*"*

Chester Bowles

Don and Janice W. came to my office visibly upset. Close to tears, Janice sat anxiously on the edge of her chair. "He called me six times at work," she said, referring to a debt collector who was harassing her over a debt. "And every time he calls, he insults me. My boss told me if I don't get my problems worked out, he's going to fire me."

"We tried to get a debt consolidation loan about a year ago," Don said, "when we first began having trouble paying our bills after I'd gotten laid off. But we were turned down. We've tried to keep up with what we owe, but it's been an uphill battle and one we're losing. What can we do? I don't want Janice to lose her job. We need her income right now while I'm looking for work! Is bankruptcy the only way to get that debt collector off our backs?"

Many laws can help protect you when you apply for or use credit, have problems paying your bills, or purchase something. However, if you're like most consumers, you don't know what they are and the legal rights they give you. That's because government at all levels does relatively little to educate us about the laws it passes. Furthermore, although the federal government and state governments, too, produce a variety of helpful, free brochures and other information written to educate consumers about their legal rights, consumers are usually unaware that this information exists and how to access it.

It takes effort to know what your legal rights are and how to protect them. But when money is tight and you have trouble paying your bills, it's especially important to educate yourself about the federal and state consumer laws that may benefit you. To help you begin that process, this chapter provides an overview of some of the most important federal consumer protection laws and how to use them. It also provides an overview of the steps you should take to resolve credit-related problems.

Direct Contact

"The best way to win an argument is to start by being in the right."
Quenton M. P. Hogg

If you have a problem with a creditor, a credit bureau, or a debt collector, or if you believe that your legal rights as a consumer have been violated, you can take a series of steps to resolve your difficulty. Each step has increasingly serious consequences for the business or organization causing the problem.

First, contact whomever you have the problem with, and try to work things out. Your difficulty may be the result of a misunderstanding, and if that's the case, you may be able to resolve your problem simply by bringing it to the attention of someone who can take care of it for you. If the problem is relatively minor, a phone call may do. If it's more serious, put your complaint in writing, and send your letter certified mail, return receipt requested. Your letter should go to whomever has decision-making authority. If you deal with a small business, that person may be the owner; for a larger business, it may be the customer relations or customer service representative or manager or a department head. If your initial efforts get you nowhere, move up the ladder, and contact the supervisor of the person you contacted initially.

If your problem is especially serious or if your problem-solving efforts have brought no success, you may even want to send a letter to the company's president. Sometimes the president of a company is more attuned to the public relations value of helping customers resolve their problems.

Keep the tone of your letter and any follow-up calls you make polite and nonaccusatory. Your letter should include the following information:

- Description of your problem. If you feel that your legal rights have been violated, explain how and why, and mention the law you believe was violated.
- Summary of what you've done so far to try and resolve the problem and the response you've gotten. Include all pertinent dates and the names of the individuals to whom you've spoken.
- Statement of how you'd like the problem resolved.
- Your account number, your address, and a telephone number where you can be reached during the day.
- Date by which you'd like a response. Two weeks is usually a reasonable timeline.

Be sure to provide copies of relevant correspondence and other documentation that can help prove your point. This includes receipts, account statements, canceled checks, contracts, and warranties. Keep the originals for yourself. Make file copies of any letters you send.

If you don't get a response by the deadline you set in your letter, call the person you wrote to and, if necessary, send a second letter. If you send the second letter, carbon copy the following: your state attorney general's office or office of consumer affairs, your congressperson, your local better business bureau or the better business bureau in the city where the company is located, and the federal agency that regulates the company you're having trouble with. See Figure 5.1 for the types of companies regulated by various federal regulatory agencies. Letting these individuals and organizations know about your problem and your unsuccessful efforts to resolve it may put pressure on the company you contact to respond to your concerns.

Another option is to involve the media. Get in touch with the editor of your local newspaper and the news director at TV and radio stations in your community. Depending on your problem—

FIGURE 5.1 Federal Regulatory Agencies to Complain to

- Complain to the Federal Trade Commission (FTC) about credit-reporting agencies, debt collectors, retail stores, finance companies, charge card and credit card companies, government lending programs, state credit unions, public utility companies, and oil and gas companies.
- Complain to the Federal Reserve Board about state-chartered banks and trust companies that are members of the Federal Reserve System.
- Complain to the Federal Deposit Insurance Corporation (FDIC) about banks that are FDIC insured, but not part of the Federal Reserve System.
- Complain to the Comptroller of the Currency about nationally chartered banks. (These banks have the word *national* in their names or *N.A.* after their names.)
- Complain to the Office of Thrift Supervision, U.S. Treasury Department, about savings and loan associations and savings banks.
- Complain to the National Credit Union Administration about federally chartered credit unions.

the more dramatic the better, for their sake—the media may be interested in doing a story on your difficulties and the unresponsiveness of the company you're dealing with. No business wants negative media attention!

If the company you have a problem with is a member of a trade or professional association, the association may sponsor a dispute resolution program designed to help resolve problems with its members using mediation or arbitration.

Before you work with one of these programs, however, be sure that you get a written explanation of the resolution process. If it involves arbitration, find out whether the arbitrator's decision is binding. Sometimes the decision is binding only on the business; other times, it's binding on both parties. Also, if arbitration is involved, find out whether the business you have the problem with will be represented by an attorney. If so, you may want to hire an attorney to represent you so you have a better chance of resolving the problem in your favor.

Another option is using an independent dispute resolution center; most medium-sized and large communities have them. Call your local or state bar association to find out whether a dispute resolution center has been established in your area. If so, and if the business you're having trouble with is local or has a local office or retail outlet, determine whether it would be willing to attend one or more mediation sessions at the center. A trained and neutral mediator will try to help negotiate a resolution that works for everyone.

Hot Tip _____

For a list of trade associations with dispute resolution programs, obtain a copy of the federal *Consumer Resource Handbook*. This handbook is free and can be ordered by writing Handbook, Consumer Information Center, Pueblo, CO 81009. For trade associations not listed in this handbook, review the *Encyclopedia of Trade Associations* in your local library. Call the association you're interested in, and find out whether it has a dispute resolution program.

State Laws

Contact your state attorney general's office or consumer affairs office to find out about any state law that applies to your problem. Often a state law enhances or supplements the protections offered by a federal law, and unless the state law conflicts with a federal law, it usually applies. These offices can also give you advice about the best course of action for your particular problem.

You may also want to file a formal complaint with the office against the business you have a problem with. If your state receives enough complaints about a particular business or type of business, it may decide to take action, although it will not act on behalf of an individual consumer. Your state may sue the business or even write a new law that addresses the problem you and others are having.

Federal Regulatory Agencies

When you have trouble resolving a consumer problem, file a formal complaint with the appropriate federal regulatory agency. Like the state agency you complain to, a federal agency won't take action on behalf of an individual consumer, but if it receives a lot of complaints about a certain company or a specific industry practice, it will investigate. Depending on the outcome of its investigation, it may take legal action against that business or industry or propose a new regulation or law.

Call the appropriate agency to learn the process for filing a formal complaint. The *Consumer Resource Handbook*, available at no charge from the federal government, includes the names, addresses, and phone numbers of these agencies and explains the responsibilities of each. This handbook should also be available at your local library.

Lawsuits

If all your efforts to resolve your problem are unsuccessful, or if a business is in blatant violation of a consumer law, you may decide it's time for legal action. If the amount of money involved is relatively small, you can probably sue the business in small claims court, and you won't need an attorney. (See Chapter 7 for a discussion of small claims court.) Otherwise, you'll need legal help. Try to find an attorney who will take your case on a *contingency* basis. That is, instead of conventional payment, the attorney agrees to take a percentage of your winnings and gets no money if you lose, although you may have to pay the lawyer's legal expenses.

Generally, when you file a lawsuit in a state or federal district court, you can sue to recover actual damages, court costs, and attorney fees, as well as punitive damages, if the court decides that the business or organization violated your rights intentionally.

The Consumer Credit Protection Act

"'Tis not knowing much, but what is useful, that makes a man wise."
Thomas Fuller

The landmark federal Consumer Credit Protection Act was passed in 1968. It is a series of laws established to set standards for how creditors should treat consumers and to require that consumers be provided with certain types of credit-related information. These laws also establish specific processes and legal mechanisms consumers must use to protect their rights if they think their rights have been violated. The Consumer Credit Protection Act includes the Fair Credit Reporting Act, the Fair Debt Collection Practices Act, the Fair Credit Billing Act, the Truth-in-Lending Act, the Equal Credit Opportunity Act, and the Electronic Funds Transfer Act. For free, helpful brochures that summarize the key provisions of each of these acts, contact the FTC by writing the Consumer and Business Education Division, Washington, DC 20580, or calling 202-326-3650.

The Fair Credit Reporting Act

The Fair Credit Reporting Act (FCRA) is discussed in detail in Chapter 7. It restricts access to the information in your credit record and gives you the right to review your credit record and to have inaccuracies corrected at no charge. It also says that negative information about your use of credit can stay in your credit record for up to seven years and that bankruptcies can be reported for up to ten years.

Access to credit records.   The FCRA states that, in general, the only reason why a business or an organization can review your credit record is if you apply to it for:

- new or additional credit;
- insurance; or
- possible employment or a promotion.

The FCRA also allows anyone with a "legitimate business need" to review your credit record. And it permits credit bureaus to provide your credit record information to government agencies under certain circumstances.

Getting a copy of your record. If you're denied credit, insurance, or employment because of information in your credit record, the FCRA gives you the right to obtain a free copy of that record from the credit bureau that reported the negative information. However, it says that you must request your free copy within 30 days of your denial. Otherwise, you must pay for the copy. Its cost is $8 unless your state has a law mandating a lower cost.

Even if you're not denied credit, insurance, or employment due to information in your credit record, it's a good idea to review your credit record at least once a year so that you know what's in it and you can be sure that all of its information is accurate and up to date. If it's not, you will want to get in touch with the appropriate credit bureau and request that changes be made. The FCRA gives you this right. Turn to Chapter 7 for an explanation of how to obtain your credit record and for other important information about credit records and working with credit bureaus.

Errors. You have the right to ask a credit bureau to verify and correct any information in your credit record that you feel is inaccurate. Once you've contacted the credit bureau in writing, the FCRA says the credit bureau must verify the accuracy of the information you question "within a reasonable period of time." Most credit bureaus try to do so within 30 days. If the reporting agency concludes that errors exist, they must be deleted from your record, and you can ask that a corrected copy of your credit record be sent to anyone who reviewed it over the previous six months.

If the creditor says that the information you question is correct, it will remain in your credit record unless you can provide additional proof that you're right. However, the FCRA gives you the right to prepare a 100-word written statement explaining why you feel your record is in error. This statement must become a permanent part of your credit record.

When you prepare your written statement, be as factual and straightforward as possible. Mention pertinent dates when you have them, and if you have any supporting documentation, indicate that it's available for review.

FIGURE 5.2   FCRA Consumer Success Stories

Following are some outcomes in actual cases heard in various state courts regarding credit bureau and credit record abuse:

- A New York court ordered a company that had secured a consumer's credit report under false pretenses to pay $15,000 in punitive damages to the consumer whose rights were violated.
- A Michigan court awarded a consumer $50,000 in punitive damages and $21,000 in attorney fees for loss of reputation, embarrassment, and humiliation in recognition of the many "subtle and indirect adverse effects upon her personal, social, and economic life" caused by a credit bureau.
- In Texas, a consumer was awarded $10,000 in actual damages for humiliation and mental distress and $4,485 in attorney fees for credit bureau errors that caused the consumer to receive three credit denials.

Your legal recourse under the FCRA.   The law gives you the right to sue a credit reporting agency or a creditor for violating your rights under the law. If you win, you can collect actual and punitive damages as well as court costs and attorney fees. Figure 5.2 summarizes some actual legal cases where consumers felt their rights had been violated and successfully prosecuted.

Other penalties.   Under the FCRA, unauthorized persons who obtain a copy of a credit report, or any credit reporting agency employee who gives a credit report to an unauthorized person, are liable for a fine of up to $5,000, one year in prison, or both.

The Fair Debt Collection Practices Act

The Fair Debt Collection Practices Act (FDCPA), which is discussed in detail in Chapter 6, regulates the behavior of debt collection agencies and attorneys who collect debts regularly as part of their practices. Figure 5.3 summarizes rights granted by the FDCPA; Figure 5.4 summarizes successful lawsuits by consumers using the law.

Your legal recourse under the FDCPA.   When a debt collector or creditor violates the provisions of the FDCPA, you have the

---

FIGURE 5.3 Consumer Rights under the FDCPA

You have the right to terminate future contacts with bill collectors and the right to stop contacts at your place of employment if they are inconvenient or prohibited by your employer. Additionally, you have the right to indicate the time of day you want to be contacted by debt collectors, the right to dispute debts, and the right to obtain verification of debts.

---

right to sue for actual damages, plus twice the amount of any associated finance charges, plus court costs and attorney fees.

The Fair Credit Billing Act

The Fair Credit Billing Act (FCBA) helps consumers promptly resolve billing problems with open-end credit accounts such as bankcards, retail charges, or lines of credit. It does not apply to billing problems with closed-end or installment accounts.

Credit card billing problems. The following types of billing problems are covered by the FCBA:

- Charges you do not understand
- Incorrectly identified charges and charges in the wrong amounts or reflecting the wrong dates
- Charges you do not believe you or an authorized user made
- Charges for goods or services you did not accept or returned
- Charges for goods different from what you ordered
- Computational errors
- Creditor's failure to credit an account properly
- Creditor's failure to send your billing statement to your current mailing address provided that in the event of an address change, you notified the creditor at least 20 days before the billing period ended

The process for resolving a problem. To activate the law's protective measures, you must write (*not* call) a creditor about a billing problem within 60 days of the postmark date of the first

---

FIGURE 5.4   FDCPA Consumer Success Stories

Following are actual cases heard in various state courts regarding abuses to consumer rights under the FDCPA:

- A New Jersey court awarded a consumer $4,000 for creditor actions that caused humiliation, emotional distress, injury to reputation and character, and extreme nervousness.
- A Pennsylvania court awarded $1,000 in actual damages to an impoverished 70-year-old woman who received a letter from a collection agency falsely threatening an imminent lawsuit over a debt. Not only did the letter cause the woman to lose sleep and weight, it caused her to borrow money and quit her job so that she could cash in her pension to pay off her debt.
- A Florida court awarded two consumers $2,500 in actual damages, $1,000 in statutory damages, and $50,000 in punitive damages for a debt collector's late-night phone calls, threats of arrest, and inappropriate contact of a third party.

---

bill reflecting the problem. Unless the problem has been resolved by the time the creditor receives your letter, the company must acknowledge its receipt within 30 days. Within 90 days, the creditor either must provide you with an explanation of why the bill is correct and provide proof if you request it or must correct the problem.

In your letter to a creditor regarding a billing problem, include your name and account number, the date, what you are disputing, and a statement of the problem. Send your letter via certified mail, return receipt requested, to the billing inquiries address listed on your bill. *Do not* send the letter in the same envelope as your payment coupon.

Hot Tip

Many consumers lose their rights under the FCBA because they call a company about a billing problem rather than writing. Only writing can activate the law's protective provisions.

While you are waiting for a response. While you wait for a response from a creditor regarding a problem with your bill:

- you do not have to pay the amount in question or any related finance charges;
- you must continue to pay on charges that are not in dispute;
- your creditor may not threaten to damage your credit record or to take legal action to get you to pay up;
- your creditor may not close your account; and
- your creditor may apply the amount in dispute against your credit limit.

If you are told there isn't a problem. Once you're notified that no problem with your bill exists, you must pay the creditor what you owe within ten days. If you don't, the FCBA says that the creditor can report your account as delinquent to credit bureaus. However, if you continue to dispute your bill and take further action to get it corrected, the FCBA states that when your creditor reports your account as delinquent, it also must indicate that you're disputing the delinquent amount.

Defective, damaged, or inferior merchandise and services. The FCBA allows you to withhold payment on defective, damaged, or poor-quality merchandise or services you pay for with a credit card. However, the law says that you must first make a serious effort to resolve the problem with the company selling the product or services.

Your rights regarding defective, damaged, or inferior goods and services are limited if you used a travel and entertainment card or a national bankcard to make your purchase rather than a card issued by the company selling the goods or services. For the FCBA to apply in such a situation, your purchase must total more than $50 and must have taken place in your state or within 100 miles of your home address.

The Truth-in-Lending Act

The Truth-in-Lending Act (TLA), which is also discussed in Chapter 8, was passed to help make it easier for you to compare your credit options so that you can make more informed credit decisions. It requires creditors to fully disclose the cost of credit before any credit transaction is finalized. The disclosure must include, among other things, the applicable interest rate or finance charge and the annual percentage rate (APR). The law also requires creditors to provide this information in clear language that most consumers can easily understand.

When your home is used as collateral.   Under the provisions of the TLA, you have three days to change your mind about certain credit transactions when your home is used as collateral. If you decide to exercise this provision, called the *right of rescission*, you must notify the creditor *in writing* that you are canceling your contract. The three-day period begins when:

- you sign the credit contract;
- you receive a Truth-in-Lending disclosure form from the creditor; and
- you receive two copies of a notice explaining your right to rescind.

The three-day period ends at midnight of the third business day following your credit transaction. (For purposes of rescission, the three days include Saturdays, but not Sundays or legal public holidays.)

The right of rescission does not apply in every case where your home is used for loan collateral. Exceptions are as follows:

- You apply for a loan to purchase or build a home.
- You consolidate or refinance a loan already secured by your home and do not borrow additional funds.
- A state agency is the creditor for the loan.

Other provisions in the TLA limit your liability in the event your credit cards are lost or stolen. They stipulate that once you notify a credit card company that your card has been lost or stolen, you do not have to pay for any unauthorized charges, and the most you have to pay for any unauthorized charges before your call is $50.

Your legal recourse under the TLA.   If a creditor fails to comply with the TLA's provisions, the law gives you the right to sue for actual damages and twice the finance charge in the case of certain credit disclosures. If you win your suit, the court can award you no more than $1,000 and no less than $100. You also collect court costs and attorney fees. Class action suits are permitted by the TLA.

The Equal Credit Opportunity Act

The Equal Credit Opportunity Act (ECOA) gives everyone the right to apply for credit and to be evaluated on the basis of their creditworthiness without consideration given to sex, race, color, national origin, marital status, or age. The legislation also states that in evaluating your credit application, a creditor cannot ignore or discount any reliable income you receive in the form of veterans benefits, welfare payments, Social Security payments, or child and spousal support, or from a part-time job.

Hot Tip _____

Anyone older than 62 years of age may not be denied credit simply due to age. Also, if you retire and are at least 62 years old, the ECOA states that a creditor can neither ask you to reapply for credit nor close your account because of your age. However, the law says that a creditor may take into account your life expectancy or collateral when considering you for credit if you are 62 years old or older.

Acceptance or denial of credit. According to the ECOA, within 30 days after you complete a credit application and the creditor has all the information needed to process the application, you must be told whether you've been approved for credit. If credit is denied, you have a right to get the denial in writing, and the creditor must either indicate why you were turned down or tell you how to get that information. These same rights apply if a creditor closes your account, refuses to increase your credit line, makes an unfavorable change in your credit terms that does not affect the majority of other account holders, or refuses to give you credit with the same or substantially the same terms as when you applied for it.

The law also says that any accounts used by both spouses or that both spouses are liable for must be reported to credit reporting agencies in the names of both the husband and the wife. This applies only to accounts opened after June 1, 1977. (See Chapter 7 for more information about the ECOA.) However, either spouse may contact creditors on accounts that the couple opened before this date and ask them to begin reporting account information in both names. Also, either spouse can contact credit bureaus and ask that they make the information part of the spouses' individual credit histories. While not obligated to do so, most creditors and credit bureaus will comply with these requests. These provisions are especially helpful to a woman who wants to build her own credit history separate from her husband's—something every married woman should do.

Your legal recourse under the ECOA.   If you believe your ECOA rights have been violated, the law says you can sue a creditor for actual damages and for punitive damages up to $10,000. If you win your lawsuit, you can also recover court costs and attorney fees.

Electronic Funds Transfer Act

The Electronic Funds Transfer Act (EFTA) protects consumers who are victimized by automatic teller machine (ATM) fraud. The law states that if someone uses your ATM card without your authorization, you are liable for only $50 if you notify your financial institution within two business days of discovering the unauthorized use. Otherwise, you are liable for up to $500. The EFTA also stipulates that if you fail to report an unauthorized use within 60 days after your bank statement has been mailed to you, you risk losing whatever is in your account as well as any remaining credit you have for overdraft protection. Figure 5.5 describes how to protect yourself from ATM fraud.

The EFTA also applies to point-of-sale terminals, telephone funds transfers, and computer transactions.

Your legal recourse under the EFTA.   If a financial institution violates the provisions of the EFTA, you may sue for actual damages and for punitive damages of no less than $100 and no more than $1,000. In certain cases, where the institution fails to correct an error or properly credit an account, you may sue for three times actual damages. Court costs and attorney fees can be collected if a suit is successful.

Also, if an institution fails to make an electronic funds transfer or fails to stop payment of a preauthorized transfer after being properly instructed to do so, you may sue for all damages that result from that failure.

FIGURE 5.5   How to Protect Yourself from ATM Fraud

- Do not write your personal identification number (PIN) in your checkbook or carry it in your wallet.
- Select a PIN that is easy to remember and different from other numbers you commonly use, such as your Social Security number or date of birth.
- Memorize your number.
- Check your bank statements promptly.
- Be wary of a person standing too close while you use an ATM. He or she may be trying to see your PIN.
- Do not lend your ATM card to anyone.

Another Important Consumer Law: The Consumer Leasing Act

Another consumer credit law you should know about is the Consumer Leasing Act (CLA). This law applies to lease agreements for property you rent for your personal, household, or family use, including furniture, appliance, and long-term car leases. It does not apply to real estate or to daily car rentals. Also, it applies only to lease agreements that last longer than four months.

The CLA says that when you consider leasing and the lease is covered by the law, you must be provided with certain written information that will help you compare the costs and terms of your lease options as well as the costs of leasing versus buying. For a detailed discussion of how the CLA applies to long-term car rentals, refer back to Chapter 4.

According to the CLA, before signing a lease agreement, you must be given a written statement of the costs of leasing, including the amount of any security deposit, the amount of each monthly payment, as well as the costs of taxes, licenses, and registration.

You must also be given certain information about the terms of the lease, including necessary insurance, guarantees, responsibility for maintenance and servicing, and purchase option.

Your legal recourse under the CLA.   If your rights under the CLA are violated, you can sue for actual damages and collect court costs and attorney fees if you win. You may also sue for 25 percent of your total monthly payments. If you win, the court will award you no more than $1,000 and no less than $100.

Blues Busters

Consumer laws were passed for your protection; however, they can't help you if you don't know that they exist or you don't understand how to use them. Exercising your rights is not always easy, nor will you necessarily get results quickly. But if you're persistent and use every resource at your disposal, you probably will be successful.

SIX

Standing at the Brink: What to Do When You're in Financial Trouble

"I know God will not give me anything I can't handle. I just wish that he didn't trust me so much."

Mother Teresa

Kathy and Bill B. looked worried as they told me what had brought them to my office. Bill worked for an electronics firm, and Kathy was a secretary in a downtown insurance company. They were upset. They told me that they had struggled for more than a year to solve their financial problems with no luck. Even though their combined salaries provided good income, they had barely enough money to cover their expenses and were beginning to get cash advances from their credit cards to pay other ongoing debts. They were not getting ahead, and any unexpected expense could be a disaster. They had no savings and lived from paycheck to paycheck. Their credit was still good, but it wouldn't stay that way for long if they continued as they were.

"We were doing fine a year ago," Bill said. "We had a nice house; we each drove a fairly new car; and we had all the major credit cards. Then my company cut overtime and reduced my hours, and money started to get

tight. I never thought there would be a time when we couldn't earn enough money to buy whatever we wanted."

Kathy said, "When I heard that there was a chance I was going to lose my job or at least have my hours cut back, I knew we had to do something. I can't take living like this. If my son gets sick, I worry that we won't have the money to take him to the doctor, and Bill has been holding off going to the dentist because we don't have the money."

I asked Kathy and Bill questions about their income, their debts, and the status of those debts. Although they were barely making it, they were not candidates for bankruptcy. They just needed some advice and help in avoiding bankruptcy and getting ahead. They also needed to know how to deal with creditors and debt collectors and where to go for help.

Today, many people live paycheck to paycheck, on the edge of financial disaster, just like Kathy and Bill. For years, we've assumed that there would always be plenty of well-paying, secure jobs and that we'd always have enough money to buy pretty much whatever we wanted. Now, those assumptions are no longer valid for a growing number of Americans. Jobs are less secure, income growth does not always keep up with inflation, and more of us choose to go it alone as small-business owners or independent contractors rather than place our trust in employers.

The previous chapters in this book have provided you with the basic financial information and skills you need to manage your finances when money is tight. The ultimate goal of those chapters is to help you pay your bills, and maybe even put money in savings, so you don't damage your credit record or get into serious financial trouble. The chapters also advise you how to increase your income so you can get beyond the paycheck-to-paycheck existence. Despite your efforts to follow the advice in those chapters, however, serious money troubles may begin to develop. If they do, it's critical that you take immediate action. Therefore, this chapter explains the signs of serious money trouble, helps you diagnose why those troubles may be developing, and provides you with advice and guidance about what to do.

How to Recognize Financial Trouble

"There comes a time in the affairs of men when you must take the bull by the tail and face the situation."
                                                            W. C. Fields

The sooner you face up to your financial troubles, the more options you'll have for dealing with them and the less damage you'll do to your credit record. To help you nip your money troubles in the bud, this section describes the signs of moderately serious and very serious financial troubles.

Signs of Moderately Serious Financial Trouble

You are in moderately serious financial trouble if you recognize the following signs in yourself:

- You're regularly late on many of your debt payments and incur a lot of late penalties.
- Your outstanding credit card balances are increasing.
- You use cash advances to pay consumer debt or for day-to-day living expenses.
- You pay only the minimums due on your credit cards.
- You're close to or exceed your credit limit on at least some of your accounts.
- You're behind at least a month on some of your accounts.
- You use savings or borrow from friends or relatives to make ends meet.

Signs of Very Serious Financial Trouble

You are in very serious financial trouble if the following signs apply to your situation:

- You are so far behind on most of your payments that you don't see how you can catch up.
- You have trouble paying even the minimums on your accounts.
- You exceed your credit limit on most of your accounts.
- You pay numerous late charges each month.
- You get phone calls and letters from creditors and debt collectors asking you to pay up.

- You always worry about how to make ends meet, and money troubles strain your marriage and other important relationships.

Assessing the Roles That Money and Spending Play in Your Life

When money troubles begin, it's important to assess why they are happening. The reasons may be obvious or not so obvious. To help you make this assessment, the rest of this section reviews the most common reasons why people get in over their heads financially. This information may be all the help you need to analyze your situation, or you may want to get the help of a financial counselor or therapist. The local office of the Consumer Credit Counseling Service (CCCS) may also be of assistance.

Following are some common reasons why you may be experiencing moderate or serious financial trouble:

Too much debt.   Your financial obligations exceed your income. Despite your efforts to live with a spending plan and to increase your income, you can't keep up with what you owe. If this is your problem, you are not alone—using too much credit is the American way. Here's evidence: During the first half of the 1990s, consumer debt grew by nearly 40 percent. Just five years ago, the average American household had two credit cards and owed slightly more than $2,300 on them. Today, those two cards have mushroomed to four, the average household owes nearly $5,000 in credit card debt, and credit card delinquencies are at a ten-year high.

Events or circumstances beyond your control.   An expensive and unforeseen emergency has sabotaged your efforts to live within your means. For example, you or another family member has been seriously injured or has become critically ill, and medical and doctor bills take everything you have, and then some.

Poor decision making.   You have made some bad financial or investment decisions. Perhaps you didn't put into practice the advice and information presented in the preceding chapters. Or maybe you thought you were being a wise consumer, but you got taken by a fraudulent money-making opportunity.

Psychological problems with money.   You have tried to live on a spending plan and to follow all of this book's advice, but you have emotional problems with money that get in the way of being a smart consumer. Those problems undermine your efforts to manage your money wisely. Some of the ways that you may misuse money follow:

- You spend money as a mood enhancer to help you overcome boredom, loneliness, feelings of inadequacy, or depression.
- You use money to give yourself a pat on the back. If you've had a hard day, you spend money to reward yourself for getting through it. If you complete an important or a difficult project, you decide that you deserve to spend some money—you earned that right.
- Rather than exercising, enjoying the company of friends, pursuing a hobby, or reading a book, you spend money as entertainment. Your definition of a good time is spending money.
- You use money as an ego booster to overcome feelings of inferiority or low self-esteem. By surrounding yourself with material possessions, eating at expensive restaurants, and taking costly vacations, you feel better about yourself. Or you spend money in an effort to buy the admiration or approval of others.

If you believe that you have emotional problems with money and want help dealing with those problems, resources are available to help you. They include professional counselors such as psychologists and psychiatrists, publicly and privately funded mental health centers, and Debtor's Anonymous (DA). DA is a nonprofit organization that uses the proven techniques and principles of Alcoholics Anonymous to help people overcome their spending problems. Through group and individual counseling, consumers are helped to understand why they overspend and are encouraged to gain control of their finances by creating and living with spending plans. Some consumers find DA's discipline, support, and sharing of experiences and insights extremely helpful in changing their relationships with money. Others combine DA with emotional counseling. Attendance at DA meetings is free. Look in your telephone directory for the Debtor's Anonymous chapter in your area. If you cannot find one, write Debtor's Anonymous, General Service Board, P.O. Box 400, Grand Central Station, New York, NY 10163-0400.

Responding to Moderate Financial Trouble

If your financial situation is moderately serious, your credit record is already being damaged, so you need to take immediate steps to avoid harming it more. To begin, stop using your credit cards, and difficult as it may be, live on cash only until you get your finances under control. Once you stop charging, it may be possible to shape up your finances simply by cutting back on your day-to-day spending for a while and using the money you save to catch up on your bills. (To help you cut back, refer to Chapter 2.) As you catch up, be sure to make all your debt payments on time because continued late payments will further damage your credit record. To generate enough income to pay off your debts as quickly as possible, you or your spouse may want to take an extra job for a while or look into working additional hours at a current job. Also, be sure that you contact the credit managers for the accounts that you're behind on and let them know what you're doing to get caught up.

Generally, it's not a good idea to borrow money from relatives or friends to get yourself out of debt. They may not be in positions to lend you the money, so asking for it could make them feel awkward or create tension. If they do lend you money, it may make things tight for them financially. However, if you end up borrowing money from a relative or friend, treat it like any other loan. Draw up a loan agreement that you both sign, and make sure the loan is secured with collateral and that the lien is properly perfected. Doing this gives the person you borrow from a better chance for getting some of the money back if later you file for bankruptcy.

If you have several delinquent accounts with one creditor—a bank, for example—talk with your banker about the possibility of refinancing those debts by collapsing them into a single loan.

Your goal in doing this should be to lower the amount of money you pay to that creditor each month by extending the length of time you have to repay what you owe. This can be a particularly attractive option if you can refinance your debts at a lower rate of interest than what you pay currently. However, if you must refinance at a higher rate of interest than what you pay now, refinancing may not be wise.

As a rule of thumb, it's usually not a good idea to trade one kind of debt for another as a way of dealing with financial troubles. However, a debt consolidation loan, or even a home equity loan, can be a reasonable option if you still have relatively good credit, your household income is stable, and you firmly resolve that once you pay off your debt with the loan proceeds, you will not let your finances get out of control again. For example, if you lost your job, but now have a new one at a good salary, or if your financial troubles were caused by an unexpected medical crisis that is now over, a debt consolidation or home equity loan may be something to consider. You might also look into a pawnshop loan for short-term help.

Hot Tip

Beware of ads for guaranteed loans. You will be charged a substantial up-front application fee in exchange for the promise of a loan. However, the company or individual you deal with will pocket your money and will never find you a loan. End of story.

Debt Consolidation Loans

A debt consolidation loan allows you to wipe out miscellaneous debt and leaves you with a single large loan to pay off instead. This kind of loan is usually unsecured and typically made for a maximum of three years. For a debt consolidation loan to be a good deal, your monthly payment on that loan should be smaller than the total of the payments you make on the individual debts you would pay off with the debt consolidation loan. Also, the interest rate on the debt consolidation loan should be lower than the rates on your miscellaneous debts.

A debt consolidation loan has two key advantages. First and most obvious, it can help you get out of debt. Second, by paying off a single large debt rather than several smaller ones, you'll be less apt to damage your credit record by forgetting to make all of the payments or making them late.

If you want to apply for a debt consolidation loan, your best bet is to contact your bank, savings and loan, or credit union. As a general rule, steer clear of finance companies or businesses that advertise debt consolidation loans. They almost always charge high rates of interest, and they may also require that you pledge your home as loan collateral. Some may also misrepresent the terms of your loan, and if you're not careful, you could find yourself in danger of losing your home. Furthermore, working with such companies can actually hurt your credit record. Many businesses will be reluctant to extend credit to you if your credit record notes that you've borrowed money from a finance company or business that specializes in debt consolidation loans because these companies are known for having lenient credit standards.

Home Equity Loans

In 1986, when changes in the federal tax laws began phasing out interest deductions on most consumer loans, other than property loans, the popularity of home equity loans grew rapidly. Not legal in all states, a home equity loan allows you to borrow money on the equity in your home. Equity is the difference between your home's current market value and the amount you owe on your home. For example, if you owe $50,000 on your home and its current market value is $100,000, your equity is $50,000. Most equity loans are made for up to 80 percent of a home's equity value, with the home used as collateral.

A home equity loan comes with either a fixed or a variable interest rate. With a variable rate, the interest rate changes as the economy changes. When the prime rate goes down, the loan rate goes down, and when the prime rate goes up, the loan rate goes up, as does the monthly amount paid on the loan. Because interest rates can fluctuate sharply and unpredictably, you may find that the variable-rate home equity loan you initially felt was the answer to your problems suddenly becomes another debt you have trouble paying off.

Some home equity loans are structured to allow for an initial series of relatively small monthly loan payments, or even interest-only payments, followed by one or more balloon payments at the end of the loan period. Credit terms like this can sound extremely attractive to anyone anxious to get out of debt. But if you use your home as collateral, before you sign any paperwork, be absolutely certain that your financial situation will be so improved by the time the balloon payments become due that you'll have no trouble making them. Otherwise, you risk defaulting on the loan and losing your home, too.

Also, keep in mind that home equity loans don't come cheap. Most likely, you will have to pay application and appraisal fees up front.

Home equity fraud.   If you shop for a home equity loan, work only with companies you know are absolutely reputable. Otherwise, you put yourself at risk of becoming the victim of home equity fraud.

Generally, the companies that perpetrate this kind of fraud are finance companies, not legitimate financial institutions. One of their salespeople may approach you about the benefits of a home equity loan, but won't make it clear that your home will be used as collateral. If you don't fully understand the terms of the loan you agree to, you may end up legally obligating yourself to monthly payments and other terms you can't meet. As a consequence, you may lose your home.

No matter what type of loan you consider, *do not* sign anything you don't read first and thoroughly understand. And *never* sign a blank form. If you want, take home a copy of the contract so you can read it at your leisure, not with someone waiting for you to sign. Ask your lawyer or a friend you trust to read it, too. Also, as a general rule, steer clear of anyone who comes to your home, calls on the phone, or contacts you by letter about a loan. Otherwise, you put yourself at risk to be victimized.

Pawnshop Loans

Don't overlook a pawnshop loan as an immediate source of money for an unexpected expense or to tide you over until the next paycheck. Pawnshops specialize in quick, small, short-term loans and don't require credit checks before they lend. Also, a pawnshop loan won't go on your credit record.

Pawnshops give cash for a wide variety of merchandise. Items most frequently pawned are tools, electronic equipment, color TVs, musical instruments (especially guitars), cameras, and

---

FIGURE 6.1   How to Get a Good Deal from a Pawnshop

- Visit pawnshops in your area to see which already have a lot of the same kinds of merchandise you want to pawn. Those that do probably will not want your items. Also, ask at the pawnshops you visit what types of items they need and can usually sell quickly.
- Take your pawnable items to several pawnshops to get the best prices.
- Work with a pawnshop that belongs to a state or national pawnbrokers association.
- Know how much your merchandise is worth and how large a loan you need before visiting any pawnshop.
- Negotiate. Don't assume that a pawnshop's first offer is its best offer.

---

jewelry. Most pawnshops hold items for 90 days. If you don't reclaim your property during that time, it will be sold.

Although it is a quick and convenient source of cash, a pawnshop loan is also expensive. For example, when you pawn an item, you generally get only about one-fourth of its new-product value, although you could get somewhat more or less, depending on its condition. Also, pawnshops charge very high rates of interest—as much as 60 percent per annum, depending on your state. So, for example, if you live in a state where pawnshops charge 120 percent per year on the money they loan and you borrow $25, to redeem that loan in a month and to get your pawned merchandise back, you must pay $30. If you wait 90 days, or the maximum amount of time, to get your item back, you pay $40—three months' worth of interest plus the cash value of the loan. Figure 6.1 gives tips for getting the best deal at a pawnshop.

Responding to Serious Financial Trouble

*"Annual income twenty pounds, annual expenditure nineteen six,
result happiness. Annual income twenty pounds, annual expenditure
twenty pounds ought and six, result misery."*

Charles Dickens

Serious financial trouble demands immediate action. First, if
you still have any credit cards, stop using them. Keep one in case
of an emergency, preferably the one with the best terms, and cut
up the rest. You need only one bankcard; any more will just be
temptations.

Hot Tip

If you cut up your credit cards, write to all of the credit card
companies to tell them that you want your accounts closed.
Request that they inform the credit bureaus they work with
that you have closed your accounts. If you don't do this,
those accounts will continue to appear on your credit
record as active accounts and can harm your record by
making it appear that you have more credit available than
you really do.

Second, contact your creditors to see whether you can negotiate new debt payment plans that will reduce your total monthly
debt payments to a level you can more comfortably manage. You
can do the negotiating yourself, or you can get help from the
CCCS office closest to you.

When you have trouble paying your bills, it's critical that *you*
take the initiative in dealing with your creditors. If you don't,
their efforts to collect what you owe them will escalate, further
damaging your credit record and disrupting your life. Instead of
friendly notices that your accounts are past due, you'll begin
receiving threatening letters. If you still don't respond, your
accounts may be turned over to debt collectors, who will increase
the pressure. And if that doesn't get you to pay up, your creditors
may begin garnishing your wages, repossessing your property,
placing liens against your real or personal property, or even taking you to court to get judgments against you. Your life will

become a financial and legal hell, and bankruptcy may become your only option.

Initiating Debt Payment Negotiations

To negotiate new debt payment plans, write to each of your creditors, directing your letter to the credit manager. Acknowledge that you're having difficulty paying your bills, then succinctly explain why and what you're doing to get your financial situation under control. Indicate your interest in working out an agreement that would allow you to pay less on your debt each month while extending the period of time you have to pay off the debt. Refer to Figure 6.2 for an example of the type of letter to send to your creditors.

Most creditors prefer that you repay your debt in full, albeit slowly, rather than have you "walk the debt" entirely or force them to incur the expense of collection or legal action against you. Therefore, assuming that what you propose is fair and reasonable, most of your creditors will be amenable to working out payment plans you can afford. However, it's unlikely that you will have much success with creditors who have already turned your accounts over to debt collectors or with whom you have long histories of late payments. Remember, the sooner you deal with your money troubles, the more options you'll have for resolving them in a manner that minimizes harm to your credit record.

Hot Tip _____

When you start the negotiation process, contact your secured or collateralized creditors first. These are the creditors to whom you have pledged personal property—property that you could lose if you can't pay your debt. Car, boat, and computer loans are common types of secured loans, as are mortgages. In addition, you may have pledged collateral to get a home improvement or vacation loan.

Before contacting your creditors, spend some time thinking about what you can realistically afford to pay out each month given your monthly net income and monthly expenses like rent, mortgage, utilities, food, day care, and insurance. Be sure to

FIGURE 6.2   Letter to Credit Manager Regarding a New Debt
Payment Schedule

Date

Address of Credit Manager

Dear Sir or Madam:

At the present time, I am having difficulty staying current with my
accounts. This is due to [explain reasons for your financial problems].

However, I am taking steps to get my financial situation under control.
These steps include: [list what you are doing—for example, second job,
cheaper apartment, spouse now working, etc.].

As part of my effort to stabilize my financial situation, I am contacting
all of my creditors to explore the possibility of negotiating reduced
monthly payment plans for my accounts. I would like to do the same
with you.

Presently, I pay you $_____ per month, and my account balance is
$_____. I would like to propose that I begin remitting to you $_____
per month at the same rate of interest as I currently pay. I realize this
will mean that it will take me longer to pay off my debt to you and that
I will pay more in finance charges; however, if my payment is lowered
as I am requesting, I will be able to stay current on all of my bills and
will be able to pay my debt to you in full.

I believe that this proposal is fair and reasonable given my current net
monthly household income of $_____ [your household income after
taxes and all deductions] and my total monthly payments of $_____ .

I look forward to discussing this request with you.

Sincerely,

Signature

budget money for unexpected expenses as well. You must be able to pay the new amounts you negotiate because it's unlikely that your creditors will give you a second chance if you can't pay the reduced amounts on time each month. If you need help budgeting or want to figure out where you might cut your expenses, turn back to Chapter 2.

Special Concerns Regarding Your Automobile

It's important to know that if you're late making your car payments or you stop making them altogether—that is, you default on the loan—your car financing agreement or the laws of your state allow your creditor to repossess your car without giving you any prior notice. (Exactly how your creditor defines *default* will be spelled out in your contract.) Also, depending on the terms of your financing agreement, if your creditor takes back the car, you may still have to pay the loan in full, plus you'll probably be liable for towing and storage costs before you can get your car back. Therefore, move the company that holds the note on your car to the top of your list when you contact your creditors about new debt payment plans.

If your creditor refuses to work with you and demands that you return your car, you can agree to a *voluntary repossession.* If you do, you reduce your creditor's repossession expenses— expenses that you are legally responsible for paying. However, most likely, you will still be liable for paying any deficiency (the difference between what you owe on the car and the car's selling price), and the repossession will probably still show up on your credit record.

Hot Tip

Don't voluntarily give up your car if you need it. For a last-ditch effort to keep it, see a bankruptcy attorney about a Chapter 13 bankruptcy reorganization. If you file this type of bankruptcy, your car payments would be lowered.

Most state laws allow repossession to occur at any time of day or night, without prior notice. Also, the creditor may come to your property to carry out the repossession. However, it may not commit a *breach of peace* by using physical force or the threat of violence to take back your car. Some states expand the definition of *breach of peace* to include taking a vehicle despite the protests of its owner or removing it from the owner's closed garage. To determine what constitutes a breach of peace in your state, call your state attorney general's office or office of consumer affairs.

Getting Your Car Back

Once your car has been repossessed, your creditor may either keep it as compensation for your unpaid debt or resell it. Legally, you must be told what will happen to your car, and if the creditor says it will keep it , not sell it, you can demand that it be sold. Selling it is a good idea if your car is worth more than what you owe on it because the sales proceeds can help reduce or eliminate your liability for any deficiency.

The sale of your car must be conducted in a *commercially reasonable manner*, which means that it must be made according to standard industry practices or in a manner considered reasonable for a given market. It does *not* mean that your creditor must get the highest possible price for the car or even a good price. If the creditor decides to sell your car at a public auction, you must be notified so that you or a friend or relative acting on your behalf can bid on it.

If your car is not sold in a commercially reasonable manner—below fair market value, for example—you may be able to use that failure as the basis for a claim against the creditor. In addition, you may be able to use it as a defense against a deficiency judgment. In this situation, get legal advice.

Whether your car is sold privately or at a public auction, you have the right to buy it back by paying the full amount you owe on it plus all expenses associated with its repossession. Also, your state may have a law that permits you to reinstate your auto loan. In other words, you could reclaim your car by catching up on all of your back loan payments and by paying the creditor's repossession expenses as well.

Your creditor cannot sell or keep any personal property that is in your car at the time it is repossessed. Should your creditor not be able to account for any of it, get legal advice about your right to compensation.

Hot Tip _____

Any improvements you make to a car, such as installing a new CD player or security system, are considered part of the car, not your personal property.

The Deficiency

The difference between what you owe on a car and what your creditor gets for selling it is called the *deficiency.* Most states allow a creditor to sue a consumer to collect the loan balance. This is called a *deficiency judgment.* To collect, however, the proper procedures for repossession and sale must be followed.

If your creditor sues you for a deficiency judgment, a court hearing will be scheduled. If this happens, check with an attorney to find out whether you have any legal grounds for contesting the judgment—for example, the creditor breached the peace or failed to resell your vehicle in a commercially responsible manner.

Figuring Out How Much You Can Afford to Pay Each Creditor

As you think about how much you can afford to give each creditor, bear in mind that *all* your creditors should get something each month and that no single creditor should receive a disproportionately large monthly sum. The amount each receives should be determined relative to the amounts you owe your other creditors. In other words, the more you owe one creditor (compared to what you owe other creditors), the larger that creditor's monthly payment.

The worksheet in Figure 6.3 can help you systematically determine the new minimum monthly payments you can afford. Copy the headings from the worksheet onto a piece of paper, and you're ready to go. Complete the appropriate information in the Name of Creditor, Total Amount Owed, and Current Minimum Monthly Payment columns. (Figure 6.3 provides sample numbers.) Next, add the numbers in the Total Amount Owed column, and write in your grand total. This figure represents the total amount of money you owe your creditors.

FIGURE 6.3   Sample Monthly Payment Worksheet

Name of Creditor	Total Amount Owed	% of Total Debt	Current Minimum Monthly Payment	Proposed New Minimum Monthly Payment
Company A	$ 5,000	50%	$275	$100
Company B	500	5	20	10
Company C	2,300	23	95	46
Company D	1,200	12	60	24
Company E	1,000	10	50	20
Grand Total	$10,000	100%	$500	$200

Calculate the percentage of the grand total that each of the amounts listed in the Total Amount Owed column represents. To perform this simple calculation, divide each of the dollar amounts in your Total Amount Owed column by the grand total. The number you get will be expressed as a decimal. Convert the decimal to a percentage by moving the decimal point two places to the right. For example, look at the sample worksheet. The consumer owes Company A $5,000. This represents .50, or 50 percent, of the consumer's grand total debt.

Now turn your attention to the Current Minimum Monthly Payment column. Add the numbers to calculate the amount of money you pay each month in minimum monthly payments. Look back over your records to determine, on average, how many dollars short of this figure you fall each month. Next, considering your current net household income and your average monthly shortfall, figure the total amount of money you can realistically pay each month to get out of debt. Note that on the sample worksheet, the consumer's current minimum monthly payments total $500. Let's assume the consumer decides that a more realistic total is $200. To determine how much of this $200 each creditor should get, the consumer simply multiplies the applicable percentages on the worksheet by $200. Under the revised debt payment plan, Company A, for example, will now receive a minimum monthly payment of $100 (50 percent of $200), while Company C will get at least $46 every month (23 percent of $200).

Negotiation Tactics and Strategies

"If at first you don't succeed, find out if the loser gets anything."

Bill Lyons

When you write to your creditors to suggest reduced minimum monthly payments, let them know that you're treating all of your creditors equally and fairly. Emphasize that no one creditor receives preferential treatment, and explain how you determined your proposed new monthly minimums.

Some of your creditors may be more difficult to work with than others. If a creditor seems reluctant to negotiate with you or wants a larger minimum monthly payment than you can afford, don't become confrontational or defensive. Instead, explain your current financial situation again, reiterate your sincere interest in paying off your debt, and politely but firmly remind the creditor that the best way for you to do that is through reduced monthly minimums.

One strategy to consider when first contacting your creditors is to offer each a minimum monthly figure that is slightly less than the amount you believe you can really afford. This approach gives you some bargaining room and increases your chances of getting revised payment amounts you can handle. For example, if the consumer profiled in Figure 6.3 has targeted a new monthly minimum of $100 for Company A, initially it may be wise to propose an amount that is perhaps 10 percent to 15 percent less than $100 and then compromise at $100. This negotiating approach can help create a win-win situation and leave everyone happy.

Once you've negotiated new payment plans with your creditors, ask each to send you a letter that states the terms of your agreement and to change the information in your account record to reflect what you've negotiated. These changes should include a new minimum monthly payment amount; an increase in the total number of payments you'll make (to compensate for the reduced amount of each individual monthly payment); and a past-due balance of zero because the revised plan should wipe your slate clean, which means you'll start anew.

It's absolutely essential that these changes be reflected in your account records because that information is sent to credit reporting agencies. To make certain the changes are carried out, review your monthly statements once the new payment plans are in effect. If the changes are not reflected, contact the appropriate creditors once more and again request that the modifications be made.

Consumer Credit Counseling Service

"Good counselors lack no clients."

William Shakespeare

The CCCS is a nonprofit organization established about 25 years ago by the National Foundation for Consumer Credit to educate, counsel, and promote the wise use of credit. The CCCS offers free or low-cost financial education and guidance to consumers. Its services include assistance to people with minor budgeting problems and to those who need debt management plans. The CCCS has more than 580 offices across the country. If you don't see a listing in your local phone book for a CCCS office, call 800-388-2227.

When a CCCS counselor helps you negotiate new debt payment plans, he or she contacts your creditors for you. Creditors know and respect the services of the CCCS, so they are often receptive to working with CCCS clients.

Hot Tip _____

Some creditors may be more willing to extend future credit if you have completed the CCCS's debt management program. They take your involvement in the program as an indication that you are serious about getting your finances under control and about paying off your debt.

After revised payment plans have been negotiated, you begin making your payments directly to the CCCS office you work with; in turn, the office pays your creditors. In other words, your creditors no longer contact you directly. Most likely, it will take two to three years for you to complete the debt repayment plans the CCCS negotiates for you. During that time, you must avoid incurring any new debt.

If no CCCS office is located close to you, contact nearby colleges, universities, military bases, credit unions, or churches to find out whether they offer any no-cost or low-cost debt counseling services. You might also call your bank for suggestions about such assistance.

For-Profit Debt Counselors

Whenever possible, negotiate with your creditors yourself, or use the services of the CCCS or another nonprofit organization in your area. But if none of these is a realistic option for you, you may have to work with a for-profit debt counselor. Avoid those that make extravagant, unrealistic promises about what they can do for you and that charge exorbitant fees for their services. Some may also offer to consolidate your debt or to arrange for a debt consolidation loan—typically at a very high rate of interest.

Before you sign any paperwork or pay any money to a for-profit debt counselor, find out all you can about the counselor. Ask for printed information explaining the counselor's services and costs. Also, ask for the names and phone numbers of several of the counselor's clients so you can talk to them.

Study carefully all of the information you're provided. Ask questions about anything you don't understand. Make absolutely certain that all charges are clearly spelled out in the printed materials you receive. If the debt counselor has no service and cost information for you to take home, if your questions are not answered to your satisfaction, or if the counselor acts evasive, *do not* sign anything and *do not* hand over any money.

If you conclude that the debt counselor's services could benefit you, and if you feel that they are affordably priced, contact your local better business bureau and your state attorney general's office or consumer affairs office. Find out whether they have records of any complaints against the counselor. If they do, look elsewhere for help.

Debt Collectors

If a creditor turns your account over to a debt collector or a collection agency, you will probably receive a letter from the collector requesting that you pay your debt and telling you what to do if you don't think you owe the money or if you dispute the amount you're supposed to owe. When a debt collector's initial contact is by telephone, the federal Fair Debt Collection Practices Act (FDCPA) requires that the call be followed within five days by a written notice stating how much you owe and to whom you owe it. The notice must also advise you of your rights under the FDCPA.

After you're contacted by a debt collector, immediately get in touch with the creditor the collector represents to see whether you can negotiate a revised debt payment plan. Realistically, however, if your account is already in collections, it's unlikely that your creditor will be especially receptive to such a proposal because, and rightfully so, the creditor will probably feel that you should have made your offer a whole lot earlier. Also, some creditors have contracts with debt collectors that prohibit the creditors from dealing with debtors directly once they've turned their accounts over to the debt collectors.

Once a debt collector contacts you about your debt, the FDCPA gives you 30 days to respond in writing if you don't believe you owe the money or if you disagree with the amount you are said to owe. In your letter, state that you refuse to pay the amount in question, provide copies of any proof you have that supports your opinion—canceled checks, receipts, and letters, for example—and demand that all collection activities cease immediately. Be sure to indicate in your letter that you are aware of your rights under the FDCPA and that you intend to use them if necessary. Include your name, your address, and all relevant account information, make a copy of the letter for yourself, and send the original to the debt collector via certified mail, return receipt requested.

After the debt collector receives your letter, the FDCPA prohibits it from communicating with you again except to tell you that it will initiate no further contact or to let you know what the next step will be if further collection action is planned. However, if the collector sends you proof of your debt, collection proceedings will resume.

Should collection proceedings move forward, deal with the debt collector calmly, rationally, and politely, realizing that emotional intimidation may be part of the collector's strategy to get you to pay up. Explain your situation, indicate your interest in paying off the debt, and explore the possibility of working out a payment plan.

Staying cool may not be easy because a debt collector's actions can sometimes be upsetting and stressful. For example, in one instance, a consumer was contacted by the same collector 20 times in one day at work. In another, a collector had other collectors in

---

FIGURE 6.4   Practical Tips for Dealing with Debt Collectors

- Use an answering machine or voice mail to screen your calls. Doing so gives you some day-to-day control over your situation.
- Record any especially abusive messages from a debt collector, and use them to take legal action.
- Don't accept collect calls from a debt collector, and don't return the debt collector's long-distance calls unless he or she leaves a toll-free number.
- Never give a debt collector your work phone number. The credit agreement you signed did not obligate you to be bothered at work or to have your boss contacted.
- In a straightforward manner, tell the debt collector what your situation is. Do not argue, bargain, or engage in a prolonged discussion.
- Do not refuse to pay a debt that you know you owe. Indicate your desire and willingness to clear up the debt even if you can't pay anything at the time of the call. Say something like, "I would really like to be able to send you the $500 I owe, but I am simply not able to do so at this time."
- If you have already explained that you can't pay your debt right away, do not talk with the collector again if he or she continues to call you.
- Keep a written record of all phone conversations you have with a debt collector, including the date and time of the call, the name of the collector, the subject of the call, and a brief summary of what was discussed.

---

his office chant in unison "pay your debt, pay your debt" each time the debtor answered his phone. Figure 6.4 summarizes a few strategies for dealing with debt collectors.

The Fair Debt Collection Practices Act

The FDCPA governs how debt collectors and collection agencies may communicate with consumers and provides legal recourse for those consumers who feel their rights have been violated under the act. Debt collectors, as defined by the FDCPA, are individuals who regularly collect debts owed by others, including attorneys who regularly handle debt collection matters as part of their practices. The law does not apply to a creditor's

FIGURE 6.5   Important FDCPA Guidelines

The FDCPA prohibits a variety of practices and actions, including the following:

- Use or threat of violence or harm to a person, property, or reputation
- Repeated phone calls to a debtor
- Threats of arrest or imprisonment (No such thing as debtors prison exists.)
- Falsely implying that a collector is a government representative or attorney
- Misrepresenting the amount of money owed by a consumer
- Depositing or threatening to deposit a post-dated check before the date on the check
- Making a debtor accept collect calls or pay for telegrams

in-house collections department. Personal, family, and household debt, including charge accounts, auto loans, and medical expenses, are all covered by the FDCPA. Figure 6.5 summarizes the protection offered by the FDCPA.

According to the law, debt collectors may contact you in person, by phone, by fax, by telegram, or through the mail. However, if they use the mail, they may not contact you with postcards that mention your debt, nor may they use see-through envelopes. They are also barred from using mailing envelopes that have return addresses or symbols that would indicate that the senders are debt collectors.

The FDCPA says that debt collectors may contact you only between 8 AM and 9 PM unless you specify that other hours of the day are better. Also, you cannot be contacted at work if collectors are aware that your employer doesn't want you being interrupted during working hours.

Unless you hire an attorney to deal with debt collectors, the collectors are free to contact people to learn where you live or work, but not for any other reason. In general, when such contacts are made, the debt collectors may not indicate that you owe money.

How to Protect Your Rights

If you feel that a debt collector has violated the provisions of the FDCPA, get in touch with the collector's manager, and try to resolve things yourself. If you can't, contact the creditor that hired the debt collector, and get in touch with your state attorney general's office or office of consumer affairs. Many states have their own debt collection laws that may provide a remedy for your problem. You may also want to file a complaint with the Federal Trade Commission (FTC). Although this agency will not take action on behalf of an individual consumer, it will take action against a company or an entire class of businesses if it gets enough complaints from consumers to establish a pattern of abuse. The FTC can also file class action lawsuits.

If you decide to take legal action against a debt collector, you have one year from the date you believe the violation occurred to file suit in state or federal court. You may sue for damages, court costs, and attorney fees.

Hot Tip _____

To file a complaint about a debt collector with the FTC, write the commission's headquarters at 6th and Pennsylvania Aves., N.W., Washington, DC 20580, or call 202-326-2222. (See Figure 7.11 in Chapter 7.) Or you may contact the appropriate FTC regional office. The addresses and telephone numbers of the FTC's regional offices may be found in the "Resources" section at the end of this book.

Finding Legal Assistance

If you need legal assistance, but can't afford to hire an attorney, check your local phone directory to see whether a legal aid office is located in your area. Such offices are partially funded by the federal government and offer free or low-cost legal help, depending on your income. If you can't find a listing for legal aid in your area, write the Legal Services Corporation, 750 1st St., N.E., 11th Floor, Washington, DC 20002-4256, or call 202-336-8800.

If you don't qualify for legal aid assistance, or if no legal aid office is convenient to you, check with your local or state bar association to find out whether it can suggest a source of affordable legal assistance. Also, a law school in your area may run a legal clinic.

FIGURE 6.6   Criteria for Selecting an Attorney

- Can I afford the attorney's rates?
- Does the attorney explain my options and potential liability in terms I understand?
- Does the attorney seem knowledgeable about the issues I face?
- Does the attorney seem sincerely interested in solving my problem, or is he or she just interested in the fee?

The Threat of Legal Action

"Next week there can't be a crisis. My schedule is already full."
Henry Kissinger

You need to meet with an attorney if you are unable to negotiate a revised debt payment plan with a creditor and legal action is threatened or if you continue to dispute the validity or amount of a debt you owe and the debt collector or creditor is talking about taking legal action.

To locate an attorney, get the names of several general practitioners (specialists are more expensive, and you probably don't need one at this point). Call them to find out whether they offer an initial free consultation; it's possible that you can get all the information and advice you need about how to deal with your problem during this first meeting. If none does, ask whether any of the lawyers would schedule an initial one-hour consultation with you and how much that meeting would cost. Attorneys' rates vary depending on their reputations, their practices, and the regions of the country in which they are located. One hour of legal advice generally ranges from $40 to $125. Figure 6.6 summarizes tips for selecting a lawyer.

If you have little or no money to spend on legal help, get in touch with one of the no-cost or low-cost sources of legal assistance previously mentioned in this chapter.

Before your first meeting, gather together any background information you have about your problem, as well as relevant correspondence, receipts, and account statements. To accomplish the maximum in the hour you'll have with the attorney, put together a list of all your questions. When formulating them, keep in mind what you want to take away from this meeting. You want to assess the seriousness of your situation and the strength of your legal position, understand what your options are and how the attorney can help, and find out what you might be able to do without a lawyer's help to resolve your problem. You especially need answers to the following questions:

- Does my problem merit the expense of an attorney?
- If the creditor or collector got a judgment against me, what would my liability be? What can they do to me?
- Am I judgment-proof?

After talking with the lawyer, you may decide that you can handle the situation yourself. However, if your potential liability is significant, you need professional help. If you do work with an attorney, be very clear about how his or her fees are structured, and find out whether the attorney would be willing to do what you need done for a set price. Also, learn whether you can defray some of your legal expenses by helping with the research, picking up or delivering documents related to your problem, or doing other work for the attorney.

If a lawsuit has already been filed against you, or if the possibility of one is very real, talk to an attorney immediately. If a lawsuit is imminent, you and your attorney should be doing everything possible to prevent it from being filed. Once it is, and once a judgment has been rendered against you, the collector's or creditor's debt collection rights increase significantly, and the collector can get a lien against your property. In addition, having a judgment against you further damages your credit record.

Your Taxes and the IRS

If you're in financial trouble, you may be unable to pay all or part of your income taxes by April 15th, the filing deadline. If you find yourself in this situation, file your tax return by the deadline anyway. In addition, get in touch with the IRS immediately to avoid a serious escalation of that agency's considerable collection powers.

Income tax extensions are extensions to file, not to pay, your taxes. Therefore, if you file an extension to buy yourself some time, the IRS still expects you to send a check or money order for what you think you will owe in taxes with your extension paper-work. If you don't, the agency will begin assessing failure to file penalties against you immediately, plus interest and other penalties such as late payment penalties. Failure to file penalties are the stiffest and are calculated monthly at the rate of 5 percent of your unpaid tax balance, with a cap of 25 percent. Interest, compounded daily, and additional penalties will continue to accrue until you've paid your taxes in full. You may also be liable for underpayment penalties. All of these penalties plus the interest you accrue will add up quickly, so it's always best to pay the IRS as soon as possible.

It's also a good idea to write a letter to the IRS requesting abatement of penalties and explaining why you're having a problem paying what you owe. In most cases, the IRS will work with you; however, any interest you owe is nonnegotiable.

A Partial Tax Payment

If you can pay only some of your income taxes, complete and mail your tax return by April 15, and include with it a check or money order for as much as you can afford. Enclose with your return a letter that briefly explains your current financial situation, indicates that what you're sending is all that you can presently afford, and promising that you'll send money each month until your taxes are paid in full. It's also a good idea to call the IRS at 800-829-1040 to convey this same information. Send your letter certified mail, return receipt requested, and keep a copy of it for your files.

If your back taxes are paid in full within a year, the IRS will take no further action, and you should receive no further communication from the agency. If at some point during that year, however, your financial situation takes a turn for the worse and as a result you realize that you will not be able to make your IRS payments, or if you need to arrange for lower monthly payments, call the IRS immediately at the number above, and request that you be referred to a problem resolution officer. As a further precaution, file Form 911, "Application for Taxpayer Assistance to Relieve Hardship." You may file this form by telephone (800-829-3676), in person, or by mail. If you don't advise the IRS of the change in your situation, the agency will treat you as though you've defaulted on your agreement, and it will begin collection proceedings.

FIGURE 6.7   Your Responsibilities under an Installment Agreement

An IRS installment agreement remains in effect *only* if the following extremely important conditions are met:

- You pay each installment on time.
- You pay all future tax liabilities on time.
- You provide the IRS with correct and complete financial information upon request.
- The IRS judges that collection of the taxes you owe is not at risk.

If any one of these conditions is not met, the IRS will notify you by mail that you are in violation of your agreement and that the agency will take enforcement action unless you pay your taxes in full immediately.

If it will take you up to 36 months to pay your back taxes, or if you owe the IRS more than $10,000, it will automatically file a lien against one or more of your assets to ensure that it will get its money if you default. This lien becomes part of your credit record, and even after you get the lien released by paying off your taxes, a record of the lien remains in your credit file for up to seven years, damaging your credit record.

Help in Developing a Payment Plan

If you want to pay your back taxes through an installment plan, but are unsure what to suggest, file your tax return by the April 15th deadline, and call 800-829-1040. You will have to provide the IRS with information about your income and expenses so it can determine what it thinks is a realistic payment plan. The monthly amount you pay will not be driven by what you owe the IRS, but rather by your current financial situation. Do not agree to larger payments than you can realistically make, since failure to live up to your installment agreement will result in an escalation of the IRS's collection proceedings, and you could experience loss of property, garnishment of wages, or other unpleasant consequences. Figure 6.7 summarizes your responsibilities under an installment agreement.

The IRS personnel you talk with about your desire for an installment plan will probably be quite helpful—unlike the stereotypical ogres you may conjure up when you think of this agency.

Remember, IRS employees are simply doing their jobs, and maybe they even experience their own financial difficulties. Be cooperative and polite when working with them, and they will probably treat you the same way.

If the IRS wants you to pay more taxes than you want to pay, or if it recommends that you sell some of your property to raise the money you owe and you balk at that suggestion, it will notify you that it plans to initiate collection proceedings. If this happens, file Form 911, and get legal advice immediately. You may need to declare bankruptcy to protect your assets from the IRS.

Failure to Contact the IRS about Unpaid Taxes

If you fail to contact the IRS about your unpaid taxes after you've filed your return, you will begin receiving a series of notices in the mail. They will come over a six-month period, and their tone and the kinds of collection actions the IRS threatens you with will grow progressively more serious. Therefore, as soon as you receive a notice from the IRS, get in touch with the agency. Don't ignore the notice. If the IRS decides that your tax debt is collectible, it will try to work out payment arrangements, possibly an installment plan. However, the longer you wait to get in touch, the less bargaining power you will have and the less amenable the IRS will be to working with you.

The first notice you'll receive will be a demand for your unpaid taxes. Ten days later, if you've not responded, you'll receive a notice that a lien may be filed against your property. If you still don't respond, you'll receive three more notices over a period of several months. After about six months, you'll receive by certified mail the agency's final notice, an intent to levy. If you don't respond to this within 30 days, the IRS will take action to collect its taxes.

Levy is a term meaning the seizure of personal property—for example, your home or your bank account—to secure payment for taxes owed. In fact, the IRS may actually come to your home to take some of your property. However, unless you're presented with a court order that gives an IRS agent access to your home, do not let the IRS agent inside.

Obviously, if the IRS threatens to levy, you're in serious trouble. Take two steps *immediately*. First, file Form 911 with your local IRS District Problems Resolution Office or Service Center to temporarily stop the seizure process and give you time to get some legal advice. You may file this form over the phone, in person, or by mail.

Second, call the number on the notice or the IRS Problem Resolution Office for your district. If you can't find this number in your local phone book, call the IRS taxpayer assistance number for your area, or call 800-829-1040.

If you're concerned that the IRS will try to seize the funds in your bank account, here are a couple of tips for protecting that money:

- When the IRS asks you for information about your bank, do not lie. However, as soon as you can, take all of your money out of your current bank, put it in another bank, and begin doing business there. That way, your old account holds no money for the IRS to take.
- To pay the IRS, open an account at a bank at which you have no other accounts. That way, if the IRS levies your account, the money it takes will have been intended for it anyway. Do not put any money other than funds earmarked for the IRS into this account.

If You Can't Pay the IRS Anything

Again, complete and mail your federal tax return by April 15th, and call 800-829-1040 to explain your situation to the IRS. The individual you speak with will ask you to complete a financial statement to determine whether you can pay anything and to ascertain whether you have any assets that you might sell or the agency might take. If the IRS determines that your account is uncollectible, collection proceedings will be suspended until your finances improve. Your situation will be reviewed in six months, and if no change has occurred, the IRS will continue to take no action. However, each year until your back taxes plus all interest and penalties are paid, you will receive a notice from the IRS reminding you of your outstanding debt.

The IRS will have up to ten years to collect what you owe. During that time, you *will* be expected to file annual tax returns. Once a return indicates that your financial situation has improved, the IRS will contact you to negotiate an installment agreement for payment of your tax liability.

Hot Tip ───────────────────────────

Put your Social Security number on any check or money order you send to the IRS. Do the same if you send the IRS a letter. After your check has cleared and is returned to you with your other canceled checks, write on it the tax period and the kind of taxes you paid.

If you receive a bill for tax penalties and you have questions about why you're being billed, contact the IRS for an explanation. The telephone number and address of the office to contact will be at the bottom of the bill. If you owe the penalties, but you have a good explanation or *reasonable cause* for why you violated IRS rules and incurred them, ask this same office how you can get the penalties waived. For example, a serious illness might be considered a reasonable cause.

The IRS and Payroll Taxes

If you're a business owner and have fallen behind on your payroll taxes, the process for getting caught up is similar to the process for paying personal tax liabilities. However, if the IRS determines that your company has a pattern of nonpayment, it will eventually shut down your business, because it will view your problem as a matter of tax abuse, not as a collections matter. If the IRS threatens to shut you down and you can't prove that you can pay your back taxes, bankruptcy is probably your best course of action.

When Bankruptcy Is Necessary

"When written in Chinese, the word crisis is composed of two characters. One represents danger, and the other represents opportunity."
John F. Kennedy

Bankruptcy should *always* be considered your remedy of last resort. However, bankruptcy *can be* your best option in some situations. For example, perhaps you're about to lose your home or your car to a creditor or the IRS or another creditor is ready to levy against your bank account, seize your property, or garnish your wages.

Bankruptcy is a legal process that either wipes out your debt or allows all or part of that debt to be repaid over a period of time, usually at a lower interest rate. Bankruptcy protects you from the IRS for up to five years, giving you time to pay your back taxes. Although bankruptcy offers you a fresh start, you may lose some of your assets, depending on the kind of bankruptcy you file. Also, your bankruptcy stays on your credit record for up to ten years, making it difficult to get new credit during this time.

Types of Bankruptcy

Four types of bankruptcy are available to consumers:

Chapter 7—straight liquidation. Under a Chapter 7 bankruptcy, most of your debt is wiped out, but you lose your nonexempt property. Each state has laws that protect certain types of property from creditors. This is your exempt property. A consumer bankruptcy attorney can tell you about the exemptions your state allows. It's important to know what they are because the exemptions will help you protect your assets from creditors. The more assets you can exempt, the less you will lose in a Chapter 7 bankruptcy. Consumers and all types of businesses can file Chapter 7.

Chapter 13—adjustment of debt. Chapter 13 allows you to reorganize your debts by lowering your monthly payments. It also protects you from the collection actions of your creditors while you pay off those debts. Exactly how the debts will be repaid is outlined in a reorganization plan developed by your attorney and based on information you provide. Your reorganization plan must be approved by the court. If you file Chapter 13, you remain in bankruptcy until all of your debt is paid off according to your plan, and you have up to five years to make all of your payments. Chapter 13 is the most popular type of individual bankruptcy, but small businesses run as sole proprietorships can also file.

Chapter 11—reorganization bankruptcy. Businesses that want to reorganize but that are not sole proprietorships must file this type of reorganization bankruptcy. Also, consumers who have too much debt to be eligible for Chapter 13 can reorganize using Chapter 11. However, in reality, given the expense and delays involved in filing a Chapter 11, most consumers and small-business owners convert their Chapter 11s to Chapter 7s.

Chapter 12—family farmer reorganization. This type of bankruptcy works much the same as Chapter 13. It was created to help farmers keep their land.

Hot Tip _____

Once you file a Chapter 13 bankruptcy, you have five years to pay the IRS what you owe, but you still must file annual tax returns. Interest and penalties will not accrue on your unpaid taxes if the IRS did not take a lien against your property before you filed for the Chapter 13.

Finding a Bankruptcy Attorney

Bankruptcy is a serious and often emotional step. Therefore, it's important that you find a skilled attorney to help you. This person should be someone with whom you feel comfortable, whom you feel will be sensitive to your concerns, and whom you feel will work hard to represent you. You also want to find an attorney whose fees are reasonable. Locating this person can be difficult, but here are some helpful tips:

- Look in the Yellow Pages of your local phone book to see whether any attorneys in your area are board-certified as bankruptcy specialists. An attorney who is board-certified in bankruptcy law should be your first choice.
- Contact lawyers who advertise. Their services may be more reasonably priced than other attorneys'. If you find a board-certified attorney who advertises, you may have a winning combination.
- Ask an attorney you know for a referral to a bankruptcy attorney.
- If you know someone who has filed bankruptcy and that person was happy with his or her attorney, get the attorney's name and phone number.
- Call the bankruptcy court in your area, and ask for the names and telephone numbers of the local bankruptcy trustees. Because trustees work in the bankruptcy system every day, they know which attorneys do the best work.

- Contact your state or local bar association. Most have lawyer referral services.
- Make appointments to see several attorneys to judge which ones best understand your problems and can express clear solutions. Comparison shop for price, too.

Hot Tip

For more information on personal bankruptcy, read my first book, *The Bankruptcy Kit: Understanding the Bankruptcy Process, Knowing Your Options, Making a Fresh Start* (Chicago: Dearborn Financial Publishing, Inc., 2nd edition). This book thoroughly explains the various types of bankruptcies and describes exactly what to expect, depending on the type of bankruptcy you file. It also explains how to find an attorney and what to expect of your attorney.

Blues Busters

When your spending plan isn't working and the debt collectors start calling, it's critical that you develop a plan of action immediately. Ignoring your financial problems or thinking that things are bound to get better if you just wait long enough will inevitably lead to financial disaster and the loss of your hard-earned assets. Therefore, at the first sign that your financial situation is getting out of control follow the advice in this chapter.

SEVEN

The Lowdown on Credit Bureaus

"It does not do to leave a live dragon out of your calculations if you live near him."

J. R. R. Tolkien

Not long ago, a bank asked me to put on a seminar for people having money troubles. I invited someone from the Consumer Credit Counseling Service (CCCS), a psychologist who specializes in helping people deal with the emotional and psychological consequences of money problems, and a representative of a major credit bureau to participate.

The seminar started off well. The presenters were well-prepared, and the consumers who attended seemed to appreciate the information they were receiving. Then the credit bureau representative began her presentation. Suddenly, angry questions abounded.

One person said he had been trying to clear up misinformation in his credit record for a year and demanded to know why it was so difficult.

Another said that errors in his credit record had delayed the processing of his mortgage loan and questioned why the credit bureau was so slow in responding to his inquiries.

171

A third asked how she could make her credit record more attractive to lenders because her credit history had been damaged by past financial difficulties.

Every question held frustration. These people were upset! It was something I had experienced before whenever the issue of credit bureaus came up.

Why do credit bureaus evoke such emotion? And why is learning how they work, what a consumer's rights are when dealing with credit bureaus, and how to make them responsive so important to everyone? The answer is that credit bureaus can affect your life in significant ways. The information they maintain about you in their files can affect your ability to get a national bankcard or a loan, rent an apartment, get the job or promotion you want, or get the insurance you need.

Credit bureaus have less influence over you if you live without credit. But that's a tough challenge in today's world and may not be realistic for many people. Therefore, like it or not, credit bureaus are a reality in your life, and to deal with them successfully, you need to understand how they work, how to read and interpret your credit report, and how to get problems in your credit file corrected. This chapter helps you do all of those things.

What Is a Credit Bureau?

Credit bureaus, or credit reporting agencies, are businesses that collect information about individual consumers and sell that information to creditors and others. Creditors use credit bureau information to help them make decisions regarding whether to extend new or additional credit to consumers.

Three national credit bureaus exist—TRW, Equifax, and Trans Union. Additionally, there are numerous local and regional credit bureaus, most of which are either owned by or affiliated with one of the nationals.

Credit bureaus maintain their consumer credit information in computerized databases. The information a credit bureau maintains on you is called your *credit history* or *credit record*. In essence, this information is a profile of your bill-paying habits—your track record as a consumer. It includes information on your debts, whether you're up to date or behind on your payments, how often you've been late paying your debts over a certain period of years, whether you've defaulted on any of your debts, whether any of your accounts has been turned over to a collection agency or debt collector, and whether a creditor has closed any of your accounts. If you've ever applied for a loan or a bankcard, at least one credit bureau maintains a file on you.

Credit bureaus obtain most of their information from the creditors who subscribe to the credit reporting services. These subscribers include lending institutions, retailers, mortgage companies, and bankcard companies. Many creditors provide consumer account information to the bureaus they work with on a monthly basis, while others report periodically, or only in the case of a default. Some creditors limit their reporting to delinquent accounts or to those in collections; others report on all accounts. Figure 7.1 summarizes subscriber reporting activity.

Credit bureaus also collect information about the consumers in their files from public records. This information includes bankruptcies, foreclosures, tax liens on property, arrests, and court judgments. In addition, when a consumer completes a credit application, information such as the consumer's name, Social Security number, marital status, present and former addresses, and employment history may go into a credit bureau's database.

Who Sees Your Credit Record?

The Fair Credit Reporting Act (FCRA) is a federal law that restricts access to consumers' credit records to help protect their privacy and gives consumers certain rights in regard to their credit histories, including the right to review their own credit records and the right to correct problems in those records.

Lenders of credit are the primary users of credit bureau information. However, they are not the only users. The FCRA says that insurance companies can also review your credit history for underwriting purposes and that employers can look at that information as part of their hiring or promotion decision-making process. Prospective landlords can also review your credit record, and under certain circumstances, government agencies can, too. For example, a government agency can review it if you apply for a special government license or for a security clearance.

In addition, the FCRA says that anyone with a *legitimate business need* can review your credit record. Because the law does not define the term, it's been broadly interpreted by the credit

---

FIGURE 7.1   Frequency of Creditor Reporting

Information on these accounts is generally reported monthly to credit bureaus:

American Express
MasterCard
Visa
Discover
Diners Club
J. C. Penney
Sears
Oil and gas credit cards
Airline charge cards
Department store and local retailer credit cards
Mortgages
Automobile loans
Student loans paid to banks
Credit union loans

Information on these accounts is generally reported only in the event of collection proceedings, a lawsuit, or a judgment:

Utility bills
Telephone bills
Medical bills
Bills from attorneys

---

reporting industry, allowing the industry to make substantial profits by repackaging consumer credit record information and selling it to direct marketers, retailers, and other commercial databases. As a result, over the past decade, credit bureaus have been widely criticized by public watchdog groups, consumers, the media, and public policymakers concerned about the buying and selling of consumers' personal information without their knowledge or their permission. They also worry about the impact of this practice on the privacy of consumers, especially now that our society is so computerized. Although numerous Congressional hearings on the subject have been held and many proposals for amending the FCRA have been introduced, to date the law has not been amended.

Some credit bureaus prepare investigative reports for insurance companies and employers. These reports include subjective information about consumers, based on interviews with people who are familiar with the consumers' lifestyles, habits, characters and reputations. If a company requests an investigative report on you, the FCRA says that you must be told immediately that it has been requested, but you don't have to be told who has requested it. However, if you're denied a job or insurance because of information in the report, the law says that the company that ordered the report must let you know that it did so and give you the name of the organization that prepared the report so you can request a copy and read what it says. You also have the right to get erroneous information in an investigative report corrected.

Why You Should Review Your Credit Record

"Bureaucracy is a giant mechanism operated by pygmies."
Honoré de Balzac

Because the information in your credit record can affect your life in many ways, it's important to know what credit bureaus say about you and how to correct any errors you find in your credit record. This is information that all consumers should have regardless of their financial situations.

During the early 1990s, credit bureaus were widely criticized because their credit reports were difficult for most consumers to understand, because their files were full of misinformation about consumers, and because consumers who discovered problems in their records often had difficulty getting the problems corrected. In response to intense public criticism and to lawsuits filed by attorneys general in many states, the credit reporting industry initiated numerous reforms. For example, it improved the readability of its credit reports and made it somewhat easier for creditors to correct credit record problems. However, a need for additional reforms remains, especially in the area of consumer privacy.

Hot Tip ————————————————————

It's a good idea to review your credit report every year to make sure that it is up to date and accurate.

How to Obtain a Copy of Your Credit Report

Because different credit bureaus get their information from different subscribers, the record one bureau maintains on you may differ from that maintained by another credit reporting agency. Therefore, you probably need to request copies of your credit report from more than one credit bureau. To start, find out which of the national credit bureaus have credit files on you, and request a copy of your credit report from each. Then move on to any local or regional credit reporting agencies not affiliated with one of the nationals.

TRW provides each consumer with one free copy of his or her credit record every year. You must pay a small fee to obtain your credit report from Trans Union and Equifax unless you're entitled to a free credit report because you were turned down for credit, employment, or insurance due to credit record information. Presently, in most states, the fee is $8 plus state sales tax.

To request your TRW report, send a signed, written request to TRW, P.O. Box 8030, Layton, UT 84041-8030.

To request a copy of your credit record from Trans Union, call 610-690-4940, and from Equifax, call 800-685-1111. The information to include in your request letters is reviewed later in this section.

To find out whether any independent local or regional credit bureau in your area maintains a credit file on you, look in your local Yellow Pages under Credit Reporting Agencies or Credit Bureaus. Call the ones listed to learn whether they're owned by or affiliated with one of the nationals. If not, ask whether you're in their databases. If you are, find out how to obtain a copy of your credit report and how much it costs.

In your credit report request letter, include your full name (including Jr. or Sr., for example), date of birth, Social Security number, spouse's full name and Social Security number (if applicable), maiden name (if applicable), current and former addresses for the past five years, and daytime and evening phone numbers, as well as a check or money order for the appropriate amount. Sign your request, and send it together with proof of your name and current address—a copy of your driver's license, a utility bill, or a bankcard billing statement, for example. Once a credit bureau receives your request, it should respond within three business days.

Hot Tip _____

If you recently applied for credit, insurance, or employment and were turned down due to information in your credit record, you're legally entitled to a free report, assuming you make the request in writing within 30 days of the credit denial. The company that turned you down is required to tell you which credit bureau to contact. Any of the three national credit bureaus will provide a free report if you make your request within 60 days of your denial.

To help you obtain a copy of your credit report, review the letters in Figure 7.2 and Figure 7.3.

How to Read Your Credit Report

Once you've obtained your credit report, read it carefully, and make certain that everything is correct and up to date. The report formats used by the major national credit bureaus are quite different. TRW presents its information in a narrative format that is easy to read and understand. Equifax does not use a narrative format, but its report is still quite readable. Also, Equifax provides a helpful explanation of how to read it. Trans Union's credit report is the most difficult to understand because it relies heavily on symbols and codes that can be confusing. But the company provides explanatory information that can help you decipher the report information.

Regardless of a report's format, all credit reports present the following types of information:

Identifying information. This information can include your name and address; your date of birth; your spouse's name and address, your place of employment; and your Social Security number.

FIGURE 7.2 Letter Requesting a Copy of Your Credit Report

Date

Address of Credit Bureau

Dear Sir or Madam:

Please send me a copy of my credit report. I provide the following information:

Full name _____

Social Security number _____

Date of birth _____

Spouse's name [if applicable] _____

Spouse's Social Security number [if applicable] _____

Current address (no P.O. boxes) _____

Former addresses for the past five years _____

_____

_____

Daytime phone number (_____) _____

Evening phone number (_____) _____

I've enclosed a check [or money order] in the amount of $ _____ in payment for the report. Please send my report to the following address [complete mailing address] _____

_____

_____

_____

Thank you for your assistance.

Sincerely,

[Signature]

FIGURE 7.3   Letter Requesting a Copy of Your Credit Report If You've Been Denied Credit

Date

Address of Credit Bureau

Dear Sir or Madam:

On [date], I was notified by [name of creditor] that I was denied credit due to information in my credit file. I therefore request a copy of my credit report and understand that no fee is associated with this request. I provide the following information:

Full name _____

Social Security number _____

Date of birth _____

Spouse's name [if applicable] _____

Spouse's Social Security number [if applicable] _____

Current address (no P.O. boxes) _____

Former addresses for the past five years _____

_____

_____

Daytime phone number (_____) _____

Evening phone number (_____) _____

Please send my credit report to the following address [complete mailing address] _____

_____

_____

_____

Thank you for your assistance.

Sincerely,

[Signature]

Credit history.   This is the heart of your credit report. It includes such information as

- each creditor's name and your account or loan number;
- type of account or loan—joint or individual;
- date the account was opened or the loan was established;
- credit limit on the account;
- current balance on the account or loan;
- account or loan payment history—the number of times payments have been late, whether the account or loan is in collections, and so on; and
- any account information you dispute.

Inquiries.   This section lists all the creditors and others who have reviewed your credit file or checked certain information in it. Some of the inquiry information is preceded by abbreviations. *PRM* indicates that your credit record was reviewed for a preapproved credit offer. *AM* indicates that your record was reviewed for the purpose of monitoring an account. *AR* shows that your record was reviewed by a creditor, possibly to help it decide whether your account should be canceled or whether you should be given additional credit.

Public record information.   Bankruptcies, foreclosures, judgments, and tax liens are all noted in credit reports. Convictions and information related to the timeliness of child support payments may also be noted.

If you're confused by anything in your credit report, call the credit bureau for help. The FCRA says that a credit bureau must make trained personnel available to answer your questions and to help you understand your credit report.

Hot Tip

For a detailed review of how to read the credit report of each of the major national credit reporting agencies, read my book *The Credit Repair Kit,* second edition, published by Dearborn Financial Publishing, Inc., 1996.

Common Errors

When you review your credit report, watch for the following common errors:

Accounts that are not yours.   Credit bureaus may confuse your credit information with information on people whose names are identical or similar to yours.

Inaccurate or incomplete information about your accounts. Since your account payment history is what creditors and others are most concerned about, make sure that information is correct and complete.

Outdated information.   The FCRA prohibits credit bureaus from reporting credit information that is more than seven years old; however, bankruptcies can stay in your credit record for up to ten years.

Inaccurate or outdated public record information.   For example, your credit record may not show that a tax lien on your property was released.

Inaccurate personal information.   Your name is misspelled, your address is inaccurate, or your Social Security number is wrong. These errors may sound relatively unimportant; in fact, they can cause your credit record information to be confused with someone else's or vice versa.

Correcting Your Credit Record

"Not everything that is faced can be changed, but nothing can be changed until it is faced."

James Baldwin

This section explains what to do if you discover an error in your credit record.

If your report came with a research request form or an investigation request form, complete it and send it to the appropriate address. You may want to send a letter with your form if you feel that you need to provide additional information, and you may also want to attach documentation that helps prove that your credit report is in error. This could include copies of canceled checks, billing statements, or receipts. Make file copies of the completed form and your letter, and send everything certified mail, return receipt requested. For an example of the type of letter to write, see Figure 7.4.

Once you've contacted a credit reporting agency about an error, the FCRA requires that it investigate the error and tell you the results of its research within a *reasonable period of time*. The three national credit bureaus and related credit bureaus try to do this within 30 days.

To conduct its research, a credit bureau contacts the appropriate creditor or public agency and asks it to verify the information you question. If the information can't be verified, or if the creditor confirms that it's wrong, the erroneous data must be deleted from your record, and you should be sent a corrected credit report. If the error is in a TRW or an Equifax report, at your request, the company will send a corrected version of your report to all creditors that reviewed your file over the past six months and to any employer that did so over the past two years. If the error is in a Trans Union report, when you complete your investigation request form, indicate the creditors and employers you want to receive corrected reports. Regardless of which credit reporting agency you deal with, always ask for written confirmation of who was sent a copy of your corrected report.

If a credit reporting agency determines that the information you dispute is correct, it remains in your record.

Hot Tip _____

When you try to get an error corrected, save all correspondence related to your efforts. This could be helpful if you're unable to resolve a credit record problem and decide to take legal action or to register a complaint with your state consumer protection office, your state attorney general's office, or the Federal Trade Commission (FTC).

FIGURE 7.4   Letter Requesting to Have an Error Corrected—Credit Bureau

Date

Address of Credit Bureau

Dear Sir or Madam:

In reviewing a copy of the credit report your company maintains on me, I found the following error[s]. [Describe each one succintly]:

_____

_____

_____

I request that you investigate this error [these errors], correct it [them], and send me a revised credit report at the following address [complete mailing address]:

_____

_____

_____

Also, please send a copy of the corrected report to any companies and individuals who have requested the report over the past six months. If you need to reach me by phone, call [telephone number, with area code].

Thank you for your prompt attention to this request.

Sincerely,

[Signature]

Full name _____

Social Security number _____

FIGURE 7.5   Criteria for Deleting Information from Credit Reports

Negative account information may be deleted from your credit record when:

- you can prove that the information is in error;
- the creditor can prove that the information is incorrect;
- the date of last activity (DLA) on the account is more than seven years old; or
- the creditor reporting the negative information doesn't have a record of it.

If a Credit Bureau Won't Correct an Error

"Victory belongs to the most persevering."

Napoleon

Although the process for correcting a credit record problem may sound quite straightforward, in fact, it can take a lot of time and effort, especially because the FCRA does not indicate how thoroughly a credit bureau must investigate a consumer's complaint. Typically, if a creditor or public agency says that the information you question is accurate, that's as far as the investigation will go unless you keep pushing. Figure 7.5 summarizes a credit bureau's criteria for deleting information.

If your initial efforts at correcting your credit record aren't successful, this section describes what to do next:

First, try to locate additional information that can help prove the error. Then send a letter to the creditor or public agency that provided the erroneous information. This letter should be similar to the one you sent to the credit bureau. Explain the error, and provide copies of any documentation that can help prove your point. In your letter, request that the creditor send written corrections to you and to all the credit bureaus it reports to, and ask for a copy of that communication. For a sample letter, see Figure 7.6.

If your problem is resolved, send a follow-up letter to all the credit bureaus the creditor reports to, and ask them to correct your credit files. This letter is extra assurance that your credit records will actually be corrected. Also, in this letter, ask that copies of your credit record be sent to any creditor that reviewed it over the past six months and to any employer that did so over

FIGURE 7.6 Letter Requesting to Have an Error Corrected—Creditor

Date

Address of Creditor

Dear Sir or Madam:

I recently received a copy of my credit report from [name of credit bureau]. In reviewing it, I noted an error relating to my account with you. I believe this information is in error for the reason[s] listed below and have included documentation that supports this contention.

[Succinctly list your reason(s).]

_____

_____

_____

I would appreciate your verifying this error [these errors] and providing the correct information to all the credit bureaus you report to, as well as to me. My mailing address is [complete mailing address]:

_____

_____

_____

If you need to speak with me, I can be reached at [telephone number, with area code].

Thank you for your assistance.

Sincerely,

[Signature]

Full name_____

Account number _____

the past two years. See Figure 7.7, for an example of the type of letter to send.

If your problem is still not resolved, the FCRA says that you have the right to prepare a written statement of up to 100 words that becomes part of your credit record.

If you're unable to correct a credit record problem, call your state attorney general's office or office of consumer affairs. Either of these offices can tell you about any state law that may be able to help you or can suggest other steps to take.

You may also want to file formal complaints with your area's Better Business Bureau and with the FTC, the federal agency responsible for enforcing the FCRA. Although that agency will not intervene on behalf of an individual consumer, it will take action against a credit bureau or a creditor if it uncovers a pattern of abuse. To register a complaint with the FTC, write to the Federal Trade Commission, Bureau of Consumer Protection, Washington, DC 20580. See Figure 7.8 for a sample complaint letter. Other options include mediation and filing a lawsuit against a credit reporting agency or creditor, possibly in small claims court.

Preparing a Written Statement for Your Credit Record

When you disagree about the accuracy of the information in your credit record and you're unable to get it corrected, the FCRA says that you can prepare a written statement of up to 100 words explaining what you think is wrong. This statement becomes a permanent part of your credit record. If you need help composing this statement, the FCRA says that the credit bureau must provide that help. Once you've prepared it, keep a copy for your files.

To make sure that creditors and employers that review your credit record read your statement, let them know about it when you apply for credit or for a job for which the screening process includes a review of your credit record, and ask them to read it. You may also want to give them copies of your statement.

How to Deal with Omissions

In reviewing your credit record, you may discover that it omits certain account information that you feel is important to the creation of a complete and accurate portrait of you as a financial manager. For example, you may have a good mortgage payment history that is not reflected in your file, or you may have had excellent credit under another name or in a different part of

---

FIGURE 7.7   Second Letter to Credit Bureau

Date

Address of Credit Bureau

Dear Sir or Madam:

Enclosed is a copy of a letter I received recently from [name of creditor] regarding erroneous information in the credit record you maintain on me. The error[s] relate[s] to my account [account number] with [name of creditor]. As you will note, the enclosed letter confirms that the information you have in my file is incorrect.

Please take all necessary steps to correct the error[s] in my record. In addition, please send a corrected copy of my credit report to me, as well as to any company or individual who requested my report over the past six months and to any employer that did so over the past two years.

Thank you for your cooperation.

Sincerely,

Full name _____

Social Security number _____

---

the country. If you discover important omissions, write to the credit bureau and request that the missing information be added to your file. Although credit bureaus are not required to add such information, they may do so for a small fee if the information you want added is verifiable.

If your credit report contains anything that you feel requires an explanation, ask the credit bureau to allow you to prepare a statement for inclusion in your file. For example, if you've been late on your account payments, you may want your file to note that the lateness is due to the fact that your employer shut down operations, that you lost your job under a corporate merger, or that your child has been seriously ill and you have mounting medical bills. Again, although a credit bureau is not required to add such an explanatory statement to your file, it may if you ask.

FIGURE 7.8 Complaint Letter to the FTC

Date

Address of the FTC
(Washington, D.C., office or regional office)

Dear Sir or Madam:

I am writing to file a formal complaint against [complete name of creditor or credit bureau], located at [complete mailing address]. My account number is [account number].

My complaint is as follows:

[Describe the sequence of events leading to your problem; include dates, actions you took to resolve the problem, and actions the creditor/credit bureau took; and state what you feel is objectionable about the company's actions. Enclose copies of any pertinent letters, receipts, or account statements.]

I believe that my rights have been violated under the provisions of the Fair Credit Reporting Act.

Sincerely,

[Signature]

Full name _____

Social Security number _____

Women and Credit Histories

Traditionally, women have faced unique challenges in regard to credit and credit records. Historically, a woman's credit history was kept in a joint file under her husband's name. If she wanted to obtain credit in her own name, and especially if she became divorced or widowed, this arrangement created problems for her because no record existed of her ever having used credit—it was all in her husband's name. This problem was addressed by the federal Equal Credit Opportunity Act (ECOA), which was passed in 1974. Among other things, this law says that for all joint accounts that both spouses use or that both are liable for, creditors must report account information to credit bureaus in the name of each spouse. However, this requirement applies only to accounts opened after June 1, 1977. (See Chapter 5 for additional details.)

Although passage of the ECOA has provided women with important benefits as consumers, it can also create problems for them. For example, if a woman's husband experiences money troubles and is unable to pay his debts, his negative credit information appears on both his and his wife's credit records. However, the ECOA says that if you can prove that you never used the account with the negative information or were not responsible for your husband's credit difficulties, the negative information may be deleted from your record. But in reality, because the ECOA is worded vaguely, women typically find it difficult to distance themselves from their husbands' financial troubles. Figure 7.9 offers women tips on protecting themselves from future credit difficulties due to divorce or widowhood.

If You Are Married

If you review your credit report and find that the accounts you share with your husband are not included, write to each of the creditors not reporting in your name and indicate that you would like all account information reported in your name as well as your husband's—for example, Robert Smith and Samantha Smith. Then wait a couple of months and recontact the appropriate credit bureaus to confirm that account information is being reported as you requested.

If before you married you had credit under a different name or in a different location, make sure that the credit bureaus maintaining reports on you have that information in their files. Also, if you marry and change your name, ask all of your creditors to begin reporting your account information under your new name.

If You Are Widowed or Divorced

If you divorce and decide to change your name, write to all of your creditors asking them to change your name on their account records so that you will continue to build a credit history for yourself under your new name.

FIGURE 7.9 Practical Ways That Married Women Can Prepare for Possible Divorce or Widowhood

- Maintain and manage your own checkbook, whether or not you work outside the home.
- If divorce appears likely, and if you don't already have credit in your own name, try to get some before you divorce.
- If your marriage is stable and divorce unlikely, build your own credit history, and make sure any account information you share with your spouse is reported to credit bureaus in both your names.
- Become actively involved in the management of your family's finances.
- Develop good money management skills.

If in reviewing your credit record you notice that some of the accounts you shared with your former or deceased husband are not in your record, write the credit bureau, and ask it to report them. While the credit bureau is not obligated to do so, it may be willing to include the accounts for a small fee. Before adding them, it will probably contact the appropriate creditors to confirm that you did in fact share the accounts with your husband or were jointly liable for repayment of the debt.

If you were a *user* on your former husband's account (that is, you used or paid on the account, but were not principally responsible for it), you may also ask the credit bureaus to make those accounts part of your credit history.

Hot Tip

In the event of a separation or divorce, protect your credit record by getting your name removed from all accounts you held jointly with your husband. You will not be liable for any charges made on the accounts after your name has been removed. This applies to women in all states except those living in community property states.

Community Property States

Community property states—Arizona, California, Idaho, Louisiana, Nevada, New Mexico, Texas, Washington, and Wisconsin—present unique challenges for men and women. In these states, a woman and her husband are legally liable for one another's debts and obligations and have joint control or ownership over all property and income earned during their marriage. Therefore, if either spouse defaults on a loan or fails to pay on a credit card, the creditor can take legal action against either the husband or the wife, and the credit records of both spouses are equally damaged.

Protecting Your Rights under the Fair Credit Reporting Act

Figure 7.10 summarizes your rights under the FCRA. If you believe that any of your FCRA rights have been violated by a credit bureau or a creditor, you can do things to protect yourself. First contact the credit bureau and creditor involved via certified letter. Figure 7.11 provides a sample letter. If the letter doesn't resolve your problem, seek the assistance of your state consumer protection office or attorney general's office. These offices should be able to advise you of any other steps you can take and tell you about any state laws that may apply to your situation.

You can sue a creditor or credit reporting agency for violating your FCRA rights. If you win, you can collect actual damages—the financial loss you suffered—as well as court costs and attorney fees. If the court decides that the FCRA violation was intentional, you can collect punitive damages. For a more complete discussion of how to protect your rights, refer to Chapter 5.

Small Claims Court

Every state allows consumers to use small claims court to try and settle legal disputes involving small debts and accounts. However, every state limits the maximum dollar amount that can be decided in small claims court; the limit varies from state to

---

FIGURE 7.10   Summary of Your Rights under the Fair Credit
              Reporting Act

- You have the right to a copy of your credit report.
- You have the right to dispute the accuracy and completeness of the information in your credit record.
- You have the right to request that a credit bureau investigate information in your record that you feel is wrong; and you have the right to have that information deleted if it is inaccurate or unverifiable.
- You have the right to have updated information in your credit record sent to any creditor who received a copy of your credit report during the past six months.
- You have the right to place a statement in your credit record if you dispute any of the information in your file.
- You have the right to privacy in terms of who may see your credit record. Access to your credit record is limited to those indicated in the FCRA.
- You have the right to know who has viewed your credit record over the past six months or over the past two years for employment purposes.
- You have the right to have negative information removed from your credit record after seven years or after ten years in the case of a bankruptcy.

---

state. The advantage of small claims court is that for a minimal expense, you can try to resolve a legal problem yourself, without the help of an attorney. Some states do not even allow attorneys to be present. A judge decides the case. Small claims courts work much like the popular television show "The People's Court."

To find out how to file a claim in your area's small claims court, look up the court in the city, county, or state section of your telephone directory. Ask the court clerk to send you information about the claims process. If you decide to use small claims court to try and resolve your legal problem, you may want to attend an actual court session so you can see the process in action. Doing so will help make you less nervous when it's your day in court.

FIGURE 7.11   Letter Regarding a Violation of Rights under the FCRA

Date

Address of Credit Bureau

Dear Sir or Madam:

I am writing because I believe that my rights as a consumer under the Fair Credit Reporting Act have been violated. [Note: You may also want to cite any applicable state laws after talking with your state attorney general's office or office of consumer affairs.] My reasons for contending this are as follows:

[Succinctly explain what has happened. Include all relevant dates, the actions you have taken to resolve the problem, the person(s) you have spoken with at the company, and the actions the company has taken. State what you feel is objectionable about the company's behavior and why you feel it is in violation of the provisions of the FCRA. Enclose copies of all relevant documentation, including correspondence, receipts, and account statements.]

If we are unable to satisfactorily resolve this problem, I will consider legal action. I am also sending a copy of this letter to the Better Business Bureau, my state's office of the attorney general [or office of consumer affairs], and the Federal Trade Commission [or the appropriate regulatory agency if your problem is with a creditor].

I look forward to hearing from you within seven working days.

Sincerely,

[Signature]

Your address_____

Daytime phone number _____

Many small claims courts require that parties to a small claims lawsuit try to resolve their problem using mediation before they see a judge. During a mediation session, a neutral third party will listen to all sides of the issue and helps everyone work toward a resolution of the problem that satisfies all of them.

Blues Busters

The information credit bureaus maintain about you can limit or expand your opportunities in life. Therefore, it's essential that you know how credit bureaus work, what your rights are when you deal with them, and how you can make sure that credit bureaus respect those rights. This is important knowledge to have if you want to be an informed consumer in control of your financial life.

EIGHT

Rebuilding Your Credit

"There is only one success—to be able to spend your life in your own way."

Christopher Morley

Filing for bankruptcy was not something that Gerald and Beth M. wanted to do, but they had no other option. However, although it required a lot of sacrifice, bankruptcy gave them an opportunity to reorganize their finances and start over. Once their bankruptcy was behind them, however, they soon discovered that rebuilding their credit history would not be easy.

Gerald, whose previous unemployment had pushed the couple into bankruptcy, was now an executive with a national retailer. Tending to three children between the ages of two and six took up most of Beth's time, although she brought in extra income by occasionally caring for other children in her home. Although Beth had tried to work outside the home, the cost of child care for the couple's three children was so high that her salary barely covered it. Therefore, Gerald and Beth had decided that the better option was for her to stay home.

When they came to see me, Gerald and Beth asked the same question nearly all of my clients ask: " How can we rebuild our credit?"

"Are you sure you want to do that?" I replied.

"We have no intention of taking on more debt than we can handle on my salary," Gerald responded. "We know what it's like not to be able to pay our bills and to be hounded by creditors and debt collectors. Once we had all the credit cards we could get, but we learned the hard way what a big mistake that was!"

"Then why do you want to rebuild your credit?"

"We've thought about that long and hard," Beth answered. "We've concluded that if we don't rebuild our credit, we will face some serious limitations in the future. For example, we need more living space, which means we will have to either add on to our current home or buy a new one. We'll need a loan to do either."

Gerald and Beth came to the same conclusion that millions of other people with damaged or ruined credit arrive at. Although living on cash is the safest way to manage money, at times, credit is necessary. For example, most consumers need credit to buy a home or car. It's neither practical nor realistic to think that the average person can save up enough money to buy these big-ticket items.

Credit bureaus are another important reason why people like Beth and Gerald want to rebuild their credit histories. As Chapter 7 discussed, your credit record may be reviewed when you apply for a new job, a promotion, or insurance, and having a bad credit history could limit your ability to get any of these things. See Figure 8.1 for a review of why to rebuild your credit.

Credit is a part of the American way of life, and if you know how to use it wisely, credit can be a positive financial tool—not something that will get you into financial trouble.

When to Start Rebuilding

"If you do not think about the future, you cannot have one."
John Galsworthy

FIGURE 8.1   Reasons to Rebuild Your Credit

You want to rebuild your credit so you can:

- finance the purchase of a home or an appropriate, reliable vehicle;
- get a job or start a business;
- have a credit card for emergencies and travel; or
- help your children pay for college.

Key rules of thumb when rebuilding your credit follow:

- Build slowly. Don't apply for a lot of credit. Whenever you apply for new or additional credit, the creditors will probably review your credit record. This will show up on your report as an inquiry. Most creditors take a negative view of a credit report with a lot of inquiries because they interpret them as a sign that you're trying to get too much credit.
- Keep the amount of credit you get to a minimum. Having a lot of credit can easily lead to abuse and a recurrence of financial difficulty.
- Pay at least the minimum due on all your accounts, and always pay on time. It's best to pay in full each month.
- Steer clear of credit repair or fix-it companies.

Once your financial troubles are behind you, it's time to start thinking about building a new credit history for yourself. Although you don't want to repeat the mistakes that contributed to your financial problems, you may need to borrow money from a bank at some point, and you will probably want a national bankcard for travel and emergencies.

Generally, your financial difficulties or your bankruptcy must be over for at least two years before a creditor will consider extending credit to you at reasonable terms. Until that point, address any problems that contributed to your financial difficulties, stabilize or increase your household income, and increase your savings—even if you're able to put away just a small amount each month. Also, request copies of your credit records from the three major credit bureaus and from any of the independent regional or local bureaus that maintain files on you. Correct any problems you find. In addition, keep trouble-free any active credit accounts you still have.

Rebuilding your credit record will take as long as two or three years. That's because you will be establishing a pattern of responsible credit use over time. As you rebuild, don't get frustrated or discouraged about how slow it's going. It will take time to create a new credit history for yourself, just as it took time to ruin your old one. Neither happens overnight.

Credit Repair Companies

Don't try to abbreviate the length of time it will take you to rebuild your credit by hiring a credit repair or credit fix-it company to help you. Although these companies make claims about their ability to erase bad credit or wipe a bankruptcy from your credit record, they can't do anything you can't do for yourself, for little or no money, under the terms of the Fair Credit Reporting Act (FCRA). Nor can they rebuild your record any faster than you can. Furthermore, their services will cost you as much as $2,000—often up front.

If you fall victim to the promises of a credit repair company despite these warnings, contact your state attorney general's office or consumer affairs office to learn whether you have any legal recourse under state law. Approximately 34 states have laws regulating the activities of credit repair companies, and some also provide legal remedies for consumers who get taken by those businesses.

Also, report your problem to the Federal Trade Commission (FTC). Although it will not take action on your behalf, it will move against a company if it receives enough complaints to establish a pattern of violations. Your complaint can help create such a pattern, and you will help save other consumers from becoming credit repair firm victims. To lodge a complaint against a credit repair company, contact the FTC, Credit Practices Division, Washington, DC 20580.

What Credit Repair Companies Do

Under the terms of the FCRA, a consumer who believes that his or her credit record contains incorrect information has the right to request that the information be changed. If the credit bureau does not verify the information within a reasonable period of time, the FCRA stipulates that the unverified information must be dropped from the consumer's credit record. Knowing this, credit repair companies often inundate credit bureaus with so many requests for verification of information in a consumer's credit record that the credit bureaus have trouble checking out all the requests in a timely manner.

Some credit repair companies also advise consumers to bargain with their creditors. For example, a credit repair company may tell a consumer with accounts in collection to pay only part of what he or she owes, and that when the consumer sends a check for that partial payment, to note on it that in exchange for accepting the check, the creditor promises to cease its collection efforts and to erase negative information about the account from the consumer's record. Creditors are under no legal obligation to accept such terms of payment.

Don't assume that if a credit repair company gives you a money-back guarantee that you're working with a reputable firm. That guarantee is nothing more than a way for the company to get your money. Typically, a credit repair firm making this kind of promise will take your money and then skip town before you have a chance to go to the legal authorities and try to get your money back. Often, it will go out of business and set up shop in a new community under a new name.

Rebuilding Your Credit

"'Tain't no use to sit and whine
'Cause the fish ain't on your line
Bait your hook an' keep on tryin',
Keep a-goin."

Frank L. Stanton

Everyone's situation is different, so no single guaranteed way to rebuild credit exists. Generally, however, your best strategy is to start the process by finding a bank that will make you a cash-secured loan—a loan collateralized with money in a savings account or a CD—and, once that loan is paid off, will make you a nonsecured loan. Working with a bank will help you develop a positive relationship with a creditor that may be able to help you

---

FIGURE 8.2   Overview of the Credit-Rebuilding Process

1. After finding a friendly banker, get a cash-secured loan, followed by an unsecured loan.
2. Apply for a secured national bankcard.
3. Apply for a retail store charge.
4. Make all of your debt payments on time and in full.
5. Monitor your credit record throughout the credit-rebuilding process.

---

down the road when you want to buy a car or a new home. Once you pay off your loans, your next step in the credit-rebuilding process is usually obtaining a secured bankcard. (If your credit record is not badly damaged, you may be able to get an unsecured bankcard; but usually, you'll have to start with a secured card.) Figure 8.2 summarizes the five steps for rebuilding credit.

Getting a Bank Loan

Finding a Friendly Banker

> *"A banker is a person who is willing to make you a loan if you present sufficient evidence to show that you don't need it."*
>
> *Herbert V. Prochnow*

Finding a banker sympathetic to your situation can sometimes be easier said than done. Banks are highly regulated businesses and are required to minimize their risk to protect their depositors' money. Federal and state bank examiners regularly review the types of loans banks make to ensure that they do not issue too many high-risk loans. Banks that do are in jeopardy of losing their charters.

The professional success of bank loan officers is partially influenced by the quality of the loans they make. If they make high percentages of good loans that generate money for their banks, they advance their careers. But if they make high percentages of bad loans, they do just the opposite. Therefore, because bank loan officers take a career risk every time they make a loan, the loan officers tend to be quite conservative in their lending decisions.

Start your search for a friendly banker by contacting a loan officer at the bank where you maintain your checking and savings accounts; however, try to have at least $500 to $1,000 in savings before you do. Tell the loan officer that you're trying to rebuild your credit after money troubles and that you'd like to get a cash-secured loan. Be sure he or she knows how much you have in savings. The banker may send you a loan application and set up a time to meet with you. If you used to have a strong relationship with your bank, and especially if your financial troubles were not due to irresponsible use of credit, but rather to problems over which you had little or no control, such as job loss in a corporate merger or downsizing, your bank may be open to working with you now that your financial situation has stabilized.

If your current bank doesn't want to talk with you about a loan, look for another bank. Two promising options include banks promoting consumer-friendly programs like debt consolidation loans and your employer's bank. If your employer is a valued bank customer, and if you're a valued employee, the bank might be willing to make you a cash-secured loan. A reference letter from your employer could be especially helpful. A third option is a close friend who is an important customer at a bank; he or she may be willing to put in a good word for you which could increase the likelihood that you'll end up with a loan.

If you can't find any bank willing to work with you, choose the bank that seemed the most encouraging, open a savings account there, and accumulate between $500 and $1,000 in the account. By doing this, you'll demonstrate just how serious you are about rebuilding your credit.

Hot Tip

When a loan officer turns you down for a loan, find out whether you can do anything to make yourself more attractive to the bank.

The First Meeting

Once you find a loan officer willing to talk, complete a loan application, and bring it with you to your appointment. Also bring a current copy of your credit record so that you can discuss it and explain any problems it may reflect.

At the meeting, explain that you're willing to do whatever is necessary to rebuild your credit. Tell the loan officer that you'd like a cash-secured loan and that after you pay it off, you want to apply for a non-cash-secured loan. Also, tell the loan officer about your long-term financial goals. For example, in the future, you may want to borrow money to help put your children through college, or you may want to buy a new home or remodel the one you're in. Also explain what caused your financial troubles and what you've done to resolve your problems and to prevent their reoccurrence. Do whatever you can to convince the loan officer that you're a good credit risk.

Finally, don't wear a lot of expensive jewelry to the appointment, and dress conservatively. Be on time for the meeting. Make a good first impression!

The Second Meeting

If things go well the first time, the loan officer probably will suggest a follow-up meeting. By then, the banker will have requested yet another copy of your credit record and checked it for signs of recurrent trouble. He or she also will want to be certain that you haven't applied for a lot of new credit.

If the loan officer agrees to make you a cash-secured loan, the loan probably will be for an amount close to what's in your savings account. You probably will be required to transfer that money into a certificate of deposit (CD) at the bank. Once you begin paying off your loan, make all payments on time.

When you pay off the loan, assuming you do so according to the terms of your loan agreement, you will have taken an important first step toward developing a new credit history, and you'll have money in savings besides.

Getting a Second Loan

After you pay off your first loan, contact the credit bureaus your bank reports to. Make sure that each one has a record of your payment history on the loan. If not, ask your loan officer to report it.

Then apply for a second loan from the same bank. A single loan won't help you establish a pattern of responsible credit use over time. You'll need to pay off at least one more loan.

FIGURE 8.3 Sources of Secured and Unsecured National Bankcards

Banks and savings and loans are not your only options when you shop for a good deal on a national bankcard. The following are other sources that sometimes provide excellent terms:

- Credit unions
- Professional and civic associations
- Labor unions

Also, consider applying for a bankcard from a bank outside your town or state. Financial institutions often solicit out-of-state or regional customers.

Depending on your income, your prior credit history, and your relationship with the bank, your second loan may not have to be cash-secured. Manage your new loan as responsibly as you did the first, and once it's paid off, make sure that your payment history on the loan is reflected in your credit record.

Hot Tip

If it has become obvious that the bank that gave you your first loan is happy to have your money in an account, but probably will not loan you money on a nonsecured basis any time soon, shop for a friendlier bank.

Getting a National Bankcard

As part of the credit-rebuilding process, apply for a secured Visa or MasterCard. Depending on your past financial difficulties, you may not be able to get an unsecured bankcard right away.

Selecting the best bankcard can be tricky, given the number of financial institutions and other sources issuing them these days and the variety of terms available. (See Figure 8.3 for a list of national bankcard sources.) Therefore, to get the best deal possible, take time to become familiar with the terminology and features in the typical bankcard offer. And remember, don't take any offer at face value—read the fine print. Common bankcard terms and features follow.

Annual fee.   This is the amount you pay each year for the privilege of having a national bankcard. Annual fees vary widely— usually $15 to $35 for regular bankcards and up to $50 for premium cards.

Some cards do not charge annual fees. If you find one of these, be sure that the issuing bank does not waive the fee for the first year only or substitute a monthly fee for the annual one. Also, check that the bank does not simply substitute a high rate of interest for an annual fee.

Interest rate.   All bankcard issuers charge interest on an account's unpaid balance. Interest rates vary depending on the issuer's terms of credit and the laws of the state where the card issuer is located. Different states set different ceilings for the maximum amount of interest that may be charged—usually between 16 percent and 20 percent. If you don't expect to pay your account balance in full each month, finding a card with a low interest rate should be a priority.

Credit limit or line of credit.   Maximum credit limits generally range from $300 to $6,000.

Grace period.   This is the approximate amount of time you have to pay your account balance in full each month before finance charges are assessed. Not all bankcards have grace periods, but the longer the grace period, the better—especially if you may not pay your account balance in full every month. In most cases, the grace period applies only if an account doesn't have a previous unpaid balance.

Transaction fee.   Some bankcards charge per-use fees for certain card features—cash advances and travelers check transactions, for example. The lower, the better.

Late payment fee.   The smaller the fee, the better.

Penalty for exceeding your credit limit.   Not all cards have this penalty. If the ones you're considering do, and if all of their other terms of credit are equal, go for the card with the lowest penalty.

Special features.   These may include personal check cashing, access to money machine networks and travelers check dispensaries, and cash advances.

Obtain one national bankcard only. Usually there is no reason for holding multiple cards; they are just temptations for abuse. Also, don't forget that every time you apply for credit, it will appear on your credit record as an inquiry. The more inquiries your report has, the less apt really important creditors, like the bank you want to lend you money for a mortgage, will be to give you credit or to give you credit with good terms.

Don't use your bankcard for frivolous purchases, just for things that are truly necessary. Also, once you've made payments on the card for several months, find out which credit bureaus the issuing bank reports to, and check with them to make certain that your account payments are now part of your credit record.

Hot Tip _____

BankCard Holders of America (BHA) is a nonprofit organization that produces a wide variety of helpful and inexpensive brochures on selecting and using credit cards. It also publishes a list of banks offering secured bankcards. To contact BHA, write to 524 Branch Dr., Salem, VA 24153, or call 800-638-6407.

How Secured Bankcards Work

Secured or collateralized bankcards were devised to help meet the credit needs of consumers with poor credit records and became popular in the late 1980s and early 1990s. You use a secured bankcard just like a regular bankcard. However, the issuer of the secured bankcard requires that you collateralize your credit purchases, either by opening a savings account or by purchasing a CD from the issuer. Then if you default on the account or are late with your payments, the bankcard issuer can protect itself by withdrawing an appropriate amount of money from your account or by cashing in your CD. On the other hand, if you make your payments on time, the money in your account remains untouched, your credit record gradually improves, and eventually, you will probably be able to obtain an unsecured national bankcard.

Selecting a Secured Bankcard

When you shop for a secured bankcard, there are issues to consider that wouldn't be of concern if you were shopping for a good deal on a traditional, nonsecured bankcard. Here are some of the questions you should ask yourself as you compare secured bankcard offers:

- How large a deposit do I have to make? Deposits generally range from a few hundred to a few thousand dollars. Because you may not have access to your deposit money while you have the card, the size of the deposit is important.
- At what rate will my deposit earn interest, and will I earn interest on the entire deposit or only a portion of it?
- Do I have to put my deposit in a savings account, or can I put it in a higher-yielding CD or money market account?
- What percentage of my deposit will be my credit line? It probably will range from 50 percent to 100 percent. In other words, if you deposit $1,000, you will have anywhere from $500 of credit (50 percent) to $1,000 of credit (100 percent).
- Can I increase my credit limit without increasing the size of my deposit, assuming I've made my payments on time? How soon after getting my card can I increase its limit?
- Can I convert my card to an unsecured bankcard, and under what conditions? Some banks permit this after one year, assuming payments have been made on time.
- How soon after my account is past due will the issuing bank apply my deposit to my account balance?
- How long after I close my account can I withdraw my deposit? The typical waiting period is about 45 days. Are other fees associated with the closing of my account?
- Are application or processing fees charged? If so, what are they?

Hot Tip _____

If you receive a phone call or mail solicitation inviting you to apply for a credit card at terms that sound unbelievably good, call your local Better Business Bureau and your state attorney general's office or office of consumer affairs to find out whether any complaints have been lodged against the company offering the card. Read the fine print in any literature and application forms.

Getting Retailer Credit

After you obtain a national bankcard and use it for several months, apply for credit from a retail store in your area. In most cases, a retail store will give you credit simply because you have the bankcard. Again, don't purchase anything frivolous with this additional credit. Buy something you truly need, and make your payments on time.

After you make payments on your *retail credit* for several months, contact the appropriate credit bureaus to make sure that these payments are reflected in your credit records. If not, take the steps necessary to get this payment information included.

Educating Yourself about Credit

"It is possible to fly without motors, but not without knowledge and skill."

Wilbur Wright

If your lack of knowledge about how to evaluate and use credit contributed to your financial difficulties, it's important that you become credit smart. To do that, you must familiarize yourself with the basic types of credit and with the credit-related terminology that you're likely to encounter. This information will help you evaluate loan and bankcard offers intelligently and identify when it's better to use one type of credit rather than

---

FIGURE 8.4 Ways to Become Credit Smart

- Enroll in a personal finance class at a community college.
- Read your local paper to find out about no-cost and low-cost personal finance seminars offered in your area.
- Ask your friendly banker to recommend courses you might take.
- Ask the librarian at your public library to suggest some books on credit and personal finance.
- Read consumer finance magazines like *Kiplinger's Personal Finance* and *Money.*

---

another. For example, when you need to borrow money to purchase something, should you apply for a bank loan, activate your checking account cash advance, or use a bankcard? Figure 8.4 suggests ways of getting this education.

Types of Credit

Three basic types of credit exist: open-end or revolving, open 30-day, and closed-end or installment.

Open-End or Revolving Credit Accounts

If your credit account is open-end or revolving, you are allowed to charge up to a certain limit or to use your line of credit up to a certain dollar amount. Each month, you are expected to pay at least the minimum amount due on your account. This minimum is a percentage of the account's outstanding balance. Examples of open-end credit include bankcards like Visa and MasterCard and secured bankcards.

Open 30-Day Credit Accounts

An open 30-day credit account allows you to charge up to your credit limit, but requires that you pay your account balance in full each month, or within 30 days of the billing date.

Examples of open-end and open 30-day accounts include:

Retail or store charge cards. Many retailers offer open-end charges. The laws of each state govern the terms of retail credit card agreements.

Travel and entertainment cards. Cards like American Express offer higher credit limits than most bankcards, but they also charge relatively high rates of interest when balances are not paid in full. Interest and penalties are limited by the laws of each state.

Oil and gas cards. These easily attainable, convenient cards often have high interest rates. Use them with care.

Closed-End or Installment Credit Accounts

Closed-end credit provides you with a fixed amount of money that must be repaid in predetermined amounts (or installments) over a specific period of time. Credit options that fall under this heading include the following loans:

Installment loans. These are commonly used to finance the purchase of relatively expensive goods and services, such as automobiles, furniture, home improvements, and major appliances. Monthly loan payments usually include principal plus interest, with interest assessed from the date the loan is made. Depending on the amount you borrow and on the health of your credit history, your installment loan may or may not be collateralized.

Mortgage loans. These large installment loans have long payback periods, up to 30 years. Monthly payments often include not only a loan's principal and interest, but also insurance and taxes on the property. The mortgaged property serves as collateral. Mortgage loans may sometimes be used to finance home improvements and can represent second and even third loans on a piece of real estate.

Home equity loans. See Chapter 6 for details.

The Truth-in-Lending Act

"`Tis not knowing much but what is useful that makes a man wise."
Thomas Fuller

The task of comparing sources of credit was made significantly easier in 1968 with the passage of the federal Truth-in-Lending Act (TLA). Among other things, the law requires all lenders to fully disclose to potential borrowers the total cost of credit or borrowing. This total cost includes interest plus all fees and must be expressed as both a dollar amount and an annual percentage rate (APR).

The TLA states that lenders must disclose this information, in addition to all other TLA-mandated information, before a consumer signs for credit. The disclosure must be in writing and must use standard terminology. See Figure 8.5 for other TLA provisions. The law is also discussed in Chapter 5.

Calculation of Interest

"When money is not a servant, it is a master."
Italian proverb

Although APR information is helpful to have, don't make credit decisions based on APRs alone. They won't tell you all you need to know, and relying only on APRs can be misleading. Consider also the factors discussed in the following section.

Loans and Other Closed-End Credit

When you consider various loan options, it's important that you take into account the total amount of interest you'll pay over the life of each loan. Although loans for the same amounts may have the same APRs, their total costs will be affected by the method each lender uses to calculate the finance charges you'll pay. When calculating interest, most lenders use one of three basic methods—simple interest, add-on interest, or discounted interest.

FIGURE 8.5   Provisions of the Truth-in-Lending Act

The TLA's provisions distinguish between open-end or revolving credit and closed-end or installment credit.

Open-End Credit

Lenders of open-end credit, such as bankcard issuers, must provide information about:

- length of the grace period;
- method used to calculate finance charges on the account; and
- all associated fees (for example, membership fee and transaction fee).

Closed-End Credit

Lenders of closed-end credit, such as banks making loans, must disclose the:

- amount of any down payment required;
- total amount to be borrowed or financed;
- repayment schedule (does not apply to housing loans), including the number and individual dollar amounts of payments and the total dollar amount of these payments;
- total amount of finance charges to be paid over the life of the loan, including all interest payments plus any additional costs such as insurance, service charges, late fees, and appraisal fees (in the case of a mortgage loan).

Simple interest.   Simple interest assumes that you pay interest only on the original amount of money borrowed—the principal—and that interest is calculated based on that portion of the original principal you still owe.

For example, assume you borrow $1,000 at 5 percent for one year. Interest on that loan using the simple interest method is $50. Therefore, at the end of the year, you pay $1,050, or the principal plus a year's worth of interest.

Many banks use a variation on simple interest called interest on the declining balance. With this method, you make periodic loan payments rather than a single payment at the end of the loan period, and you pay interest on the amount of the original loan principal that has not yet been repaid. The amount of interest paid decreases with each loan payment. At the same time, the amount of the original loan principal remaining for your use also gets smaller. This interest calculation method is more expensive than simple interest because you don't have full use of the money borrowed for the entire period of the loan.

For example, assume you borrow the same $1,000 at 5 percent for one year, but you pay off the loan in two payments—the first after having the loan for six months, and the second at the end of the loan period, or at the end of the year. The total amount of interest that you pay is $37.50. The first payment is $500, or half of the $1,000 plus $25 in interest (5 percent of $1,000 divided by 2, or one-half of a year). Then at the end of the year, you pay $512.50 ($500, or the balance of the loan, plus 5 percent of that balance for a half-year, or $12.50).

Add-on interest.   A lender that uses this method calculates interest on the full amount of the principal and then adds that amount to the principal. The lender then determines the amount of your payments by dividing the interest plus principal by the number of payments you make over the life of the loan. When you make two or more payments, this method is quite expensive because you don't have full use of the principal for the total period of the loan. In fact, as the number of loan payments increases, so too does the effective interest rate on the loan because you have increasingly less of the original principal to use. This method is often used by finance companies and is sometimes used by banks for consumer loans.

For instance, assume you take on the same loan amount and interest rate as in the prior two examples, and assume you make two equal loan payments over the one-year period. Using this method, you pay $525 at the end of the first six-month period ($1,050 divided in half) and $525 at the end of the year, or loan period. The effective interest rate using this method is 6.6 percent rather than 5 percent because you don't have full use of the $1,000 for the full year. Instead, $1,000 is available for the first half of the year, while only slightly more than $500 is available during the second half of the year.

Discounted interest.   When a creditor uses this method, it calculates the total amount of interest to be paid on your loan, deducts that interest amount from the loan principal, and gives you the difference. Generally, this method is used for relatively short-term loans.

Again, making the same assumptions about the amount and terms of a loan as were made in the previous examples, you actually receive $950 ($1,000 less 5 percent interest on the principal, or $50). If you repay the $1,000 at the end of the year, the effective rate of interest on the borrowed money is about 5.3 percent, slightly more than the interest paid using the simple interest calculation. Again, this is because you don't have full use of the borrowed $1,000.

Bankcards and Other Open-End Credit

When comparing open-end credit options, be aware of the method each creditor uses to calculate the balance upon which your finance charges will be calculated. This method can significantly affect the amount of interest you pay, even if the APR is the same for each credit option.

Balances for finance charges can be calculated in three different ways:

Adjusted daily balance.   This is generally your best deal. The balance is calculated by taking an account's opening balance, subtracting all payments made during the grace period, then applying the finance charge to that new or adjusted balance. New purchases made during the billing period are not included in this balance calculation.

Average daily balance.   This method is the one most frequently used by creditors. It monitors an account's balance each day during the billing period, subtracting payments and adding new purchases, in some instances. At the end of the billing period, the daily ending balances are totaled, then divided by the number of days in that period to determine the account's average daily balance.

Previous balance.   This method is generally your worst deal. Finance charges are applied to an account's previous balance without reducing that balance by the amount of payments made during the current billing period; however, new account transactions are not accounted for either.

Hot Tip _____

From a practical perspective, the total amount of your monthly payment is an extremely important consideration when you shop for credit. That's because you don't want to have problems making your payments. Two sources of credit may have the same APRs, but different payback periods. Although the source with the longer payback period will cost you less on a month-to-month basis, it's the more costly source of credit over the long term because you will pay more in finance charges. However, even if it has a higher APR, the credit with the longer payback period may be your best option if you need to keep your monthly payments as small as possible.

Home Mortgages

Qualifying for a home mortgage loan after serious financial difficulty may not be easy, but it isn't impossible—even in the case of bankruptcy. For example, you may qualify for a Federal Housing Administration (FHA) loan even if you've been out of bankruptcy only for one year, and you may be able to obtain a VA loan after you've been out of bankruptcy for two to three years.

HUD Homes

U.S. Department of Housing and Urban Development (HUD) homes are foreclosed homes that were originally financed with FHA–insured mortgages. An excellent source of well-priced real estate, HUD offers single-family homes, condominiums, and town houses. Sold "as is," the average HUD home sells for $40,000. If you are willing to buy a fixer-upper, you can get an especially good bargain.

Aside from price, the major advantage of a HUD home when you're recovering from serious money troubles is that your down payment will be smaller than if you were buying a traditional home. When you purchase a home, your up-front costs usually include earnest money or a deposit on the home to demonstrate that your offer is serious; a down payment; and closing costs. When you buy a HUD home, your deposit typically ranges from $500 to $2,000, and your down payment may be as little as 3 percent of the selling price, compared to a down payment of 10 percent to 20 percent for a traditional home. However, if you make only a 3 percent down payment, HUD will not cover such prepaid costs as taxes, insurance, and private mortgage insurance (PMI). Regardless of the size of your down payment, HUD will pay most of your closing costs, which generally run 3 percent to 4 percent of a home's price, and up to 6 percent of other costs, including your broker's fee. HUD requires the use of a real estate broker.

To find out about the HUD homes for sale in your area, look in your local newspaper's real estate classifieds section or call an area REALTOR®. Real estate brokers who sell HUD homes maintain a complete list of available HUD properties.

When you speak with a broker, ask whom to contact for loan information. If possible, get prequalified for a loan to speed up the loan process after you find a home. This is important because once you make an offer on a HUD home and your offer is accepted, you have only 60 days to close the sale. Most lenders need three to six weeks after receipt of your application to complete the loan approval process.

Completing an Application for Credit

When you fill out a credit application, be accurate and thorough; however, present your financial information in as flattering a light as possible. As you list your debts, put those with the best payment histories first. Don't omit debts with negative histories— the creditor will find out about them when it runs a credit check. In fact, omitting such information could jeopardize your chance of getting the credit you want because your honesty and integrity may be called into question. A better approach is to talk with the creditor about anything negative in your credit history or to attach an explanatory note to your application.

When listing your assets on the application, be as complete as possible, and be sure to value them at their current market values. Some of these assets may be potential collateral and could help you get the credit you want.

What Do Creditors Look for When Evaluating a Credit Applicant?

Creditors look at three basics when deciding whether to give you credit:

Capacity.   Creditors judge your ability to repay your debt by looking at your monthly income and current obligations. They use this information to calculate how much you have left over each month after you pay your bills. A rule of thumb many creditors use is that your monthly credit payments, including credit cards, should not exceed 10 percent of gross household income or 15 percent of net income, after housing and taxes. Also, most creditors don't like to extend credit to anyone whose mortgage exceeds 28 percent of his or her gross income.

Character.   Creditors evaluate your character by reviewing your credit record, together with any other information that might be relevant. In general, they believe that the way you've handled your credit in the past indicates your future credit-handling behavior, or character. This is why they usually run a credit check on you.

Collateral.   Creditors care about your collateral because they want to be sure that if you default on your loan, you have sufficient resources to back it up. Having enough collateral can often make the difference between getting and not getting the credit you need.

The Scoring Process

Most creditors use an internal scoring system to evaluate the information on your credit application and in your credit report, assigning numerical values to specific types of information. For example, if you own a home, maintain savings and checking accounts, and have a stable source of income, you will probably score higher than someone who rents, has no savings, and has just begun a business. These days, most creditors use computers to help them determine whether to approve your credit application. If you're turned down for credit by one creditor, don't lose heart—apply with another. Because every creditor uses a different scoring system, you may score higher with the next creditor you apply with.

Hot Tip _____

Some creditors give special consideration to consumers who have gone through the debt management program of the Consumer Credit Counseling Service (CCCS) and who have paid off all their debt. However, working with the CCCS is not a *guarantee* of credit.

When applying for credit that you really need, it's always a good idea to attach a letter explaining why you got into financial trouble, what you've done to deal with your financial problems, and the progress you've made. You may also want to attach letters of recommendation from your banker and from creditors with whom you have good payment histories. Figure 8.6 provides general advice on what to do before you sign a credit or loan application.

The Equal Opportunity Act

The federal Equal Credit Opportunity Act (ECOA) prohibits creditors from discriminating on the basis of sex, age, race, nationality, religion, and marital status, among other factors. It also requires that a creditor notify you in writing whether you've been granted or denied the credit you applied for. This must be done within 30 days of the time the creditor receives your credit application and all other information it needs to process it. If you're denied credit, the creditor must either tell you why or inform you of your right to know. You then have 60 days to submit a written request asking for an explanation. For more information on this law, return to Chapter 5.

Blues Busters

Although it's safest to live on a cash only basis, in our society, that's simply not practical. Therefore, this chapter has explained how to rebuild your credit after it's been damaged by serious

---

FIGURE 8.6 What to Do before You Sign a Credit Application or Loan Agreement

- Read everything—even the fine print—carefully and completely. If you have questions, get them answered to your satisfaction before you sign.
- Do not sign any blank forms that the creditor says it will fill out later. If you do, you may discover that the blanks are filled in with terms other than those you agreed to.
- If you need time to think over the credit terms, don't let the creditor talk you into signing the paperwork. It's possible that while you're off mulling things over, the paperwork will be processed, obligating you to the terms of the contract.
- If you discuss changes to be made to the contract, do not sign until the new paperwork accurately reflects the credit terms you agreed to.
- Make sure that any carbon copies attached to the paper you sign match the first sheet.
- Get a copy of all documents you sign, and file them for safekeeping.

---

money troubles. It has also cautioned against getting too much credit because for many people, multiple credit cards or big lines of credit can be prescriptions for financial disaster. Don't buy more on credit than you can afford. Use credit to purchase big-ticket necessities only or to help pay for genuine emergencies. Pay off your debt as quickly as you can; it's expensive and dangerous to carry balances from month to month. And always save as much as you can. Money in savings helps prepare you for the unexpected.

RESOURCES

When you live paycheck to paycheck, you need to be informed about how to manage your finances wisely so you can make smart choices when it comes to spending and credit. Doing so will help you stay out of financial trouble. This section refers you to books, magazines, newspapers, and other publications, as well as to organizations that can help you deal successfully with your current financial situation and create a more positive financial future. It also directs you to resources that can help you deal with financial troubles. Resources are listed under the following categories:

- Maintaining a positive attitude and developing a healthy relationship with money
- Dealing with debt
- Rebuilding credit and using it wisely
- Credit records and credit bureaus
- Living on less
- Medical expenses
- Money management
- Children and money
- Automobiles
- Careers and job hunting
- Self-employment
- Protecting your rights
- Additional resources

Maintaining a Positive Attitude and Developing a Healthy Relationship with Money

Books

Breakthrough Thinking, by Gerald Nadler, Prima Publishing, 1990.
Couples and Money, by Victoria Felton-Collins, Bantam Books, 1990.
Creative Visualization, by Shakti Gawain, Bantam Books, 1983.
The Feeling Good Handbook, by Dr. David Burns, Dutton, 1995.
Feeling Good: The New Mood Therapy, by Dr. David Burns, Avon, 1992.
Getting Off the Merry-Go-Round: You Can Live without Compulsive Habits, by Carla Perez, M.D., Impact Publications, 1994.
How to Get Out of Debt, Stay Out of Debt and Live Prosperously, by Jerrold Mundis, Bantam Books, 1990.
How to Meditate: A Guide to Self-Discovery, by Lawrence L. LeShan, Bantam Books, 1984.
How to Stop Fighting about Money and Make Some, by Adriane Berg, Avon, 1989.
Living through Personal Crisis, by Ann Kaiser Stearns, Ballantine Books, 1984.
Money Is My Friend, by Phil Laut, Ivy Books, 1990.
Necessary Losses, by Judith Viorst, Fawcett Gold Medal, 1987.
Penny-Pinching Hedonist: How to Live Like Royalty with a Peasant's Pocketbook, by Shel Horowitz, Accurate Writing, 1995.
Streamlining Your Life, by Stephanie Culp, Writers Digest Books, 1991.
Who Do You Think You Are? How to Build Self-Esteem, by Joel Wells, Thomas More Press, 1989.

Organizations

Debtors Anonymous
(For more information, see same entry under "Dealing with Debt")
Lutheran Social Services. Many communities have a Lutheran Social Services office. Emotional counseling is one of this organization's many services. The services are offered on a sliding fee scale and are available to anyone regardless of religion.

Dealing with Debt

Books

The Bankruptcy Kit: Understanding the Bankruptcy Process, Knowing Your Options, Making a Fresh Start, by John Ventura, Dearborn Financial Publishing, Inc., 1996.
Conquer Your Debt, by William Kent Brunette, Prentice Hall Press, 1990.
Debtors' Rights: A Legal Self-Help Guide, by Gudrun M. Nickel, Sphinx Publishing, 1996.

Getting to Yes: Negotiating Agreement without Giving In, by Roger Fisher and
William Ury of the Harvard Negotiation Project, Penguin, 1991.
How Anyone Can Negotiate with the IRS—and Win! by Daniel J. Pila, Winnows
Publications, St. Paul, 1990.
How to File for Bankruptcy, by Stephen Elias, Albin Renauer, and Robin Leonard,
Nolo Press, 1991.Out
How to Get Out of Debt and Live Prosperously, by Jerrold Mundis, Bantam Books,
1990.
Life after Debt, 2nd edition, by Bob Hammond, Career Press, 1996.
Money Troubles: Legal Strategies to Cope with Your Debt, by Robin Leonard, Nolo
Press, 1995.
*Out of Debt: How to Clean up Your Credit and Balance Your Budget while Avoiding
Bankruptcy,* by Robert Steinbeck, Bob Adams, Inc., 1989.
*The Ultimate Credit Book: How to Double Your Credit, Cut Your Debt and Have a Life-
time of Great Credit,* 2nd edition, by Gerri Detwiller, Plume, 1996.
Winning the IRS Game: Secrets of a Tax Attorney, by Frederick W. Daily, Dropzone
Press, 1990.

Brochures and Handbooks

From BankCard Holders of America (BHA):
Getting Out of Debt, $1
Managing Family Debt, $1
To order, write to the BHA, 524 Branch Dr., Salem, VA 24153.

Organizations

Consumer Credit Counseling Services (CCCS)
This nonprofit organization provides no-cost and low-cost financial counseling
to consumers and sponsors seminars on topics related to money management.
The CCCS has nearly 600 offices across the country. For the office nearest you,
call 800-388-2227.

Debtors Anonymous
General Service Board
P.O. Box 400
Grand Central Station
New York, NY 10163-0400
212-642-0710

Debtors Anonymous helps consumers overcome problems with spending and
debt using the proven techniques and principles of Alcoholics Anonymous. The
organization has chapters across the country. If you cannot find one close to
you, contact the organization in New York City.

Rebuilding Credit and Using It Wisely

Books

Credit Card Secrets You Will Surely Profit From, by Howard Strong, Boswell Corporation, 1989.
How to Borrow Money and Use Credit, by Martin Weiss, Forms Manual, 1990.

Brochures and Handbooks

From BankCard Holders of America (BHA):
Credit Repair Clinics: Consumers Beware, $1
How to Re-establish Good Credit, $1
Secured Credit Cards: Selecting the Best One for You, $1
To order, write to the BHA, 524 Branch Dr., Salem, VA 24153.

From the Federal Trade Commission (FTC):
Choosing and Using Credit Cards
Credit Repair Schemes
Fix Your Own Credit Problems
To order your free copies, write to the FTC, Office of Consumer and Business Education, Bureau of Consumer Protection, Washington, DC 20580.

This is just a sampling of the many publications available free of charge from the FTC. To request a listing of its publications, write to the address above. You can also read the full text of the FTC's publications by going to CONSUMER.FTC.GOV on the Internet or to its Web site at http://www.ftc.gov.

Newsletters and Magazines

BankCard Consumer News, BankCard Holders of America (BHA). Published six times a year, this newsletter is free to members. (See below for more information.)

Organizations

BankCard Holders of America (BHA)
524 Branch Dr.
Salem, VA 24153
800-638-6407

This nonprofit organization is dedicated to educating consumers about credit. The BHA publishes a variety of informative brochures, a bimonthly newsletter, and lists of national bankcards and their terms of credit. The publications are free to BHA members and available to nonmembers for small fees. Membership is $24 each year.

Credit Records and Credit Bureaus

Books

Credit Improvement Handbook, by James L. Bandy and Robert A. Freiheit, Coastline Associated Enterprises, 1986.
The Credit Repair Kit, 2nd edition, by John Ventura, Dearborn Financial Publishing, Inc., 1996.
Credit Secrets: How to Erase Bad Credit, by Bob Hammond, Paladin Press, 1989.

Brochures and Handbooks

From BankCard Holders of America (BHA):
Credit Check-up Kit, $2
Credit Secrets Manual, $1
Understanding Credit Bureaus, $1
To order, write to the BHA, 524 Branch Dr., Salem, VA 24153.

From the Federal Trade Commission (FTC) in cooperation with the Associated Credit Bureaus, Inc., the National Foundation for Consumer Credit, the U.S. Office of Consumer Affairs, and the Consumer Information Center:
Building a Better Credit Record: What to Do, What to Avoid
To order this free publication, write to the FTC, Public Reference, Washington, DC 20580.

Organizations

Associated Credit Bureaus, Inc.
1090 Vermont Ave., N.W., Suite 200
Washington, DC 20005-4905
202-371-0910

This national trade association publishes a variety of brochures related to credit and credit bureaus. Write to the association for a price list.

Living on Less

Books

How to Live within Your Means and Stay Financially Secure, by Robert A. Ortaldo, Fireside Books, 1990.
Living Well or Even Better on Less, by Ellen Kunes, Putnam Publishing Company, 1991.
The Money Diet, by Ginger Applegarth, Penguin Books, 1995.
Penny Pinching: How to Lower Your Everyday Expenses without Lowering Your Standard of Living, by Lee and Barbara Simmons, Bantam Books, 1991.

The Wholesale-by-Mail Catalog, by Lowell Miller and Prudence McCullough, The Print Project, Harper & Row Publishers, 1994.

Newsletters and Magazines

The Tightwad Gazette. This monthly newsletter has ceased publication, but three volumes of compiled issues (*The Tightwad Gazette I, II* and *III*) are available for $11.95 each in bookstores or from *The Tightwad Gazette,* RR1, Box 3570, Leeds, ME 04263, or call 207-524-7962.

Organizations

Catholic Charities. Catholic Charities agencies provide counseling, food, and housing to people in need throughout the United States. Look in your local directory for the Catholic Charities office nearest you.

United Way. Local chapters of United Way publish free directories of social welfare and medical services in their areas that could benefit people in financial difficulty. Look in your telephone book for the United Way in your community. Some United Ways cover multicommunity areas, so if you don't see a listing in your town's telephone book, look for listings in the telephone books of towns near you.

Medical Expenses

Books

Health Care Rights, by Nancy Levitin, Esq., Avon Books, 1996.
Managed Care and You: The Consumer Guide to Managing Your Health Care, by Michael E. Cafferky, McGraw-Hill, Inc., 1995.

Brochures and Handbooks

From the Health Insurance Association of America:
Guide to Health Insurance
To order a free copy, write to the Health Insurance Association of America, 5555 13th St., N.W., Washington, DC 20030, or call 202-824-1600.

From the People's Medical Society:
Getting the Most for Your Medical Dollars, $12.95 for members and $15.95 for nonmembers.
150 Ways to Be a Savvy Medical Consumer, $5.95 for members and $4.95 for nonmembers.
To order, write to the People's Medical Society, 462 Walnut St., Allentown, PA 18102, or call 800-624-8773.

Organizations

People's Medical Society
462 Walnut St.
Allentown, PA 18102
610-770-1670

This nonprofit citizens' action group works to achieve better and less expensive medical care for consumers. The People's Medical Society also educates consumers about health care and medical insurance through a variety of publications. Annual membership is $20 and includes a subscription to the *People's Medical Society Newsletter* and discounts on publications. Publications are also available to nonmembers.

Money Management

Books

The Bank Book: How to Revoke Your Bank's "License to Steal," by Ed Mrkvicka, Jr., Harper Perennial, 1994.
The Easy Family Budget, by Jerald W. Mason, Houghton Mifflin Company, 1990.
How to Live within Your Means and Stay Financially Secure, by Robert A. Ortaldo, Fireside Books, 1990.
Making the Most of Your Money: A Comprehensive Guide to Financial Planning, by Jane Bryant Quinn, Simon & Schuster, 1991.
The Only Investment Guide You'll Ever Need, by Andrew Tobias, Bantam Books, 1983.
Personal Finance for Dummies, by Eric Tyson, IDG Books Worldwide, Inc., 1995.
Sylvia Porter's New Money Book for the 80s, by Sylvia Porter, Avon Books, 1980.
Terry Savage Talks Money: The Common-Sense Guide to Money Matters, by Terry Savage, Dearborn Financial Publishing, Inc., 1990.
Your Wealth Building Years: Financial Planning for 18- to 38-Year-Olds, by Adriane Berg, Newmarket, 1995.

Brochures and Handbooks

From the American Bankers Association:
Bank Book
Managing Your Checking Account
To order your free copies, write to the American Bankers Association, 1120 Connecticut Ave., N.W., Washington, DC 20036, or call: 202-663-5087.

From BankCard Holders of America (BHA):
Money Management Guide, $5.00
To order, write to the BHA, 524 Branch Dr., Salem, VA 24153.

From the Federal Reserve Bank of Chicago:
ABCs of Figuring Interest

To order this free publication, write to the Public Information Center, Federal Reserve Bank of Chicago, P.O. Box 834, Chicago, IL 60690.

From the Federal Trade Commission (FTC):
Getting a Loan: Your Home as Security
Home Financing Primer
Mortgage Money Guide
To order your free copies, write to the FTC, Office of Consumer and Business Education, Bureau of Consumer Protection, Washington, DC 20580.

This is just a sampling of the many publications available free of charge from the FTC. To request a listing of its publications, write to the address above. You can also read the full text of the FTC's publications by going to CONSUMER.FTC.GOV on the Internet or to its Web site at http://www.ftc.gov.

From the Institute of Certified Planners:
Your Child's College Bill: How to Figure It . . . How to Pay for It
To order your free copy, write to the Institute of Certified Planners, 3801 E. Florida, Suite 708, Denver, CO 80201.

From the U.S. Department of Housing and Urban Development (HUD):
A Home of Your Own
HUD Homebuying Guide
To order, write to the Department of Housing and Urban Development, Public Information, 451 Seventh Street S.W., Washington, DC 20410.

Newsletters and Magazines

Bottom Line/Personal. Published twice monthly, this newsletter is dedicated to helping busy people manage their lives more effectively by providing them with information on a variety of important topics, including money management, taxes, careers, financial planning, and medical care. To order, write to *Bottom Line/Personal*, Subscriptions Dept., P.O. Box 58446, Boulder, CO 80322.

Consumer Reports, Consumers Union. This monthly magazine provides information and advice on consumer goods and services, health, and personal finance. It accepts no advertising. To subscribe, write to *Consumer Reports*, Subscriptions Dept., P.O. Box 53017, Boulder, CO 80321-3017.

Financial World. Published since 1902, this magazine provides advice on financial matters such as taxes, investing, and insurance. To subscribe, write to *Financial World*, P.O. Box 420142, Palm Coast, FL 32412-9554.

Kiplinger's Personal Finance Magazine. This monthly magazine covers a wide range of subjects related to money management and smart spending. To subscribe, write to *Kiplinger's*, Subscriptions Center, 3401 East-West Hwy., Editors Park, MD 20797-8203.

Money. This monthly magazine covers a variety of issues related to money, including jobs, investment, money management, and taxes. To subscribe, write to *Money*, P.O. Box 61790, Tampa, FL 33661-1790.

The Pocket Change Investor, Good Advice Press. The newsletter covers topics related to consumer finance. To order, write to *The Pocket Change Investor*, P.O. Box 78, Elizaville, NY 12523, or call 914-758-1400.

Companies, Organizations, and Miscellaneous Resources

American Association of Retired Persons (AARP)
601 E St., N.W.
Washington, DC 20049
202-434-2277

AARP is the nation's leading organization for people age 50 and older. In addition to its activities in the areas of legislative advocacy, informative programs, and community services, it publishes a variety of publications related to credit and money management that are of value to people of all ages. Additionally, AARP sponsors the Women's Financial Information Program (WFIP), a seven-week program designed to help midlife and older women develop money management skills and decision-making confidence. Offered nationally, the program is sponsored by AARP and local organizations such as YMCAs, community colleges, and women's groups.

Consumers Union
101 Truman Ave.
Yonkers, New York 10703-1057
914-378-2000

Consumers Union publishes *Consumer Reports* as well as other sources of information on consumer goods and services, health, and personal finance.

National Consumers League
1701 K. St., N.W., Suite 1200
Washington, DC 20005
202-835-3323

This nonprofit organization works on behalf of consumers. It publishes a monthly newsletter and a variety of consumer guides and brochures. Annual membership is $20.

Children and Money

Books

Fast Cash for Kids: 101 Money-Making Projects for Young Entrepreneurs, by Noel Drew and Bonnie Drew, Career Press, Inc., 1995.
The Kids' Complete Guide to Money, by Kathy S. Kyte, Knopf, 1984.
Start Your Own Lemonade Stand, by Steve Caney, Workman Publishing, 1991.
Kiplinger's Money-Smart Kids (and, Parents too!), by Janet Bodnar, Kiplinger Washington Editors, Inc., 1993.
Mom, Can I Have That? by Janet Bodnar, Kiplinger Washington Editors, Inc., 1996.
Raising Money-Wise Kids, by Judith Briles, Northfield Publishing, 1996.

Brochures and Handbooks

From the Federal Reserve Bank of New York:
Series of comic books about finance-related subjects such as inflation, banks, credit, and money.

To order your free set, write to the Federal Reserve Bank of New York, Public Information Dept., 33 Liberty St., New York, NY 10045, or call 212-720-6130.

From Fidelity Investments:
Kids and Money and You and Money: A Learning Unit for Children
To order your free brochure, call Fidelity Investments at 800-544-6666.

Magazines

"Teaching Your Kids about Money," *Money,* March 1990. For article reprints, call 212-522-5454.
Zillions, Consumers Union. To order this bimonthly magazine call 914-378-2000.

Automobiles

Brochures and Handbooks

From BankCard Holders of America (BHA):
Your Next Car: Leasing vs. Buying. What's Best for Consumers,
To order, write to the BHA, 524 Branch Dr., Salem, VA 24153.

From the Federal Trade Commission (FTC):
Buying a Used Car, 1989
A Consumer Guide to Vehicle Leasing
New Car Buying Guide
Vehicle Repossession
To order your free copies, write to the FTC, Office of Consumer and Business Education, Bureau of Consumer Protection, Washington, DC 20580.

This is just a sampling of the many publications available free of charge from the FTC. To request a listing of its publications, write to the address above. You can also read the full text of the FTC's publications by going to CON-SUMER.FTC.GOV on the Internet or to its Web site at http://www.ftc.gov.

From the National Automobile Dealers Association (NADA):
Your Money, Your Car
To order your free copy, write to the NADA, 8400 Westpark Dr., McLean, VA 22102, or call 800-252-6232.

From the National Vehicle Leasing Association (NVLA):
A Consumer Education Guide to Leasing vs. Buying
To order your free copy, write to the NVLA, P.O. Box 281230, San Francisco, CA 94128-1230.

Careers and Job Hunting

Books

The Career Finder: Pathways to Over 1,500 Entry-Level Jobs, by Dr. Lester Schwartz and Irv Brechner, Ballantine Books, 1990.

Getting Hired in the 90s, by Vicki Spina, Dearborn Financial Publishing, Inc., 1995.

Knock 'em Dead: The Ultimate Job Seeker's Handbook, by Martin J. Yate, Adams Publishing, 1994.

The 90 Minute Résumé, by Peggy Schmidt, Peterson's Guides, 1992.

The 100 Best Jobs for the 1990s and Beyond, by Carol Kleiman, Dearborn Financial Publishing, Inc., 1992.

The Perfect Résumé, by Tom Jackson, Doubleday & Co., 1992.

The Résumé Catalog: 200 Damn Good Examples, by Yana Parker, Ten Speed Press, 1988.

The Résumé Writer's Handbook, by Michael Holley Smith, Harper Collins, 1994.

Sweaty Palms: The Neglected Art of Being Interviewed, by H. Anthony Medley, Ten Speed Press, 1992.

Top Secret Résumés and Cover Letters, by Steven Provenzano, Dearborn Financial Publishing, Inc., 1995.

What Color Is Your Parachute? by Richard Nelson Bolles, Ten Speed Press, 1993.

The Whole Career Sourcebook, by Robbie Miller Kaplan, AMACOM, 1991.

Newsletters and Magazines

Federal Jobs Digest, Break Through Publications. This comprehensive biweekly lists federal job openings. To subscribe, write to *Federal Jobs Digest,* 325 Pennsylvania Ave., S.E., Washington, DC 20003, or call 800-824-5000.

Home Office Computing Magazine. This monthly magazine addresses a wide range of subjects relevant to home-based businessowners and selects the most appropriate computer technology and software. To subscribe, write to *Home Office Computing Magazine,* P.O. Box 53561, Boulder, CO 80322, or call 800-678-0188.

National Business and Employment Weekly. Published by *The Wall Street Journal,* this newspaper features job ads as well as information and advice on landing a job. To subscribe, write to *The Wall Street Journal,* 200 Burnett Rd., Chicopee, MA 02120, or call 800-562-4868.

Self-Employment

Books

The Entrepreneur Magazine Small Business Answer Book, by Jim Schell, John Wiley & Sons, Inc.

Good Idea! Now What? by Howard Bronson, Bestsell Publications, 1988.

Homebased Businesses, by Beverly Neuer Feldman, Fawcett-Crest, 1989.

Home Business Resource Guide, by Cheryl Gorder, Blue Bird Publishing, 1989.

How to Become Successfully Self-Employed, by Brian R. Smith, Adams Publishing, 1994.

How to Make Nothing but Money: Discovering Your Hidden Opportunities for Wealth, by Dave Del Dotto, Warner, 1991.

How to Start Your Own Business for $1,000 or Less, by Will Davis, Upstart Publishing Co., 1995.

The McGraw-Hill Guide to Starting Your Own Business: A Step-by-Step Blueprint for the First-Time Entrepreneur, by Stephen C. Harper, McGraw-Hill Publishing Co., 1991.

Moonlighting: 148 Great Ways to Make Money on the Side, by Carl Hausman and the Philip Lief Group, Avon Books, 1989.

One Hundred Best Home Businesses for the 90s, by Paul and Sarah Edwards, J. P. Tarcher, 1991.

184 Businesses Anyone Can Start and Make a Lot of Money, by Chase Revel, Bantam Books, 1984.

Strategic Planning for the New and Small Business, by Fred L. Fry and Charles R. Stoner, Upstart Publishing, Inc., 1995.

Steps to Small Business Startup, by Linda Pinson and Jerry Jinnett, Upstart Publishing Co., 1996.

Working from Home: Everything You Need to Know about Living and Working under the Same Roof, by Paul and Sarah Edwards, Putnam Publishing Group, 1994.

Your First Business Plan, 2nd edition, by Joseph Corello and Brian Hazelgren, Sourcebooks, Inc., 1995.

Brochures and Handbooks

From the U.S. Department of Commerce (DOC):

Directory of Federal and State Business Assistance: A Guide for New and Growing Companies

To order, write to the DOC, National Technical Information Service, Springfield, VA 22161, or call 703-487-4650.

The U.S. Small Business Administration (SBA) publishes a variety of publications, videotapes, and workbooks about financial management, professional management, planning, and marketing for small businesses.

For a list of its publications and tapes and for ordering information, write to The SBA, Office of Business Development, 409 Third St., S.W., Washington, DC 20416, or call 800-U-ASK-SBA.

Organizations

Mothers' Home-Business Network
P.O. Box 423
East Meadow, NY 11554
516-997-7394

This national support group provides information for women who want to successfully combine motherhood with home-based businesses. A $35-per-year membership buys a quarterly newsletter as well as several publications.

National Association for the Self-Employed
Member Services
P.O. Box 612067
DFW Airport, TX 75261
800-232-6273

A business support group for the self-employed, this organization provides its members with access to group insurance and discounts on travel and office equipment. It also offers a toll-free business advice hot line. Membership is $72 each year.

Protecting Your Rights

Books

Everybody's Guide to Small Claims Court, by Ralph Warner, Nolo Press, 1995.

Brochures and Handbooks

From BankCard Holders of America (BHA):
Consumer Credit Rights, $1
Credit Card Fraud, $1
Solving Your Credit Card Billing Questions, $1
Women's Credit Rights, $1
To order, write to the BHA, 524 Branch Dr., Salem, VA 24153.

From the Board of Governors:
Consumer Handbook to Credit Protection Laws
To order your free copy, write to the Board of Governors, Federal Reserve Board, Publications Services, MS-127, Washington, DC 20551, or call 202-452-3000.

From the Federal Financial Institutions Examination Council:
Consumer Rights
To order your free copy, write to the Federal Financial Institutions Examination Council, 2100 Pennsylvania Ave., N.W. Suite 200, Washington, DC 20037.

From the Federal Trade Commission (FTC):
Equal Credit Opportunity
Fair Credit Billing
Fair Credit Reporting
Fair Debt Collection
Fix Your Own Credit Problems
Solving Credit Problems
To order your free copies, write to the FTC, Office of Consumer and Business Education, Bureau of Consumer Protection, Washington, DC 20580.

This is just a sampling of the many publications available free of charge from the FTC. To request a listing of its publications, write to the address shown. You can also read the full text of the FTC's publications by going to CON-SUMER.FTC.GOV on the Internet or to its Web site at http://www.ftc.gov.

From the U.S. Office of Consumer Affairs:
Consumer Resource Handbook
To order your free copy, write to Handbook, Consumer Information Center, Pueblo, CO 81009, or call 719-948-3334.

This is an excellent resource that every consumer should have. Updated annually, it provides the names, addresses, and phone numbers of federal, state, and local consumer protection agencies, corporate consumer contacts, and selected federal agencies.

Newspapers and Newsletters

Nolo News, Nolo Press. Published quarterly, this publication provides practical legal advice and information on consumer issues, updates on consumer laws, and ordering information for books published by Nolo Press. For a free sample, call 800-992-6656.

Additional Resources

The Consumer Information Catalog describes all of the free or inexpensive brochures published by the federal Consumer Information Center. The center's brochures cover a wide range of subjects of concern to consumers, including cars, credit, employment, federal benefits programs, housing, money, and small business. To order this free catalog, write to the U.S. Government Printing Office, Superintendent of Documents, Public Documents Distribution Center, Pueblo, CO 81009. You can also review the publications available through this source by going to its Web site at http://www.pueblo.gsa.gov.

Federal Information Centers (FICs) located in each state will answer your questions about government programs, services, laws, and regulations that affect you or will direct you to someone who can. Call 301-722-9098 for the phone number of the FIC closest to you. Users of TDD/TTY throughout the United States may call 800-326-2996.

INDEX

Start Enjoying Greater Financial Freedom
Triple Your Investment Portfolio

SAVE Thousands on Real Estate as a Buyer or Seller